Dividend Stocks

A Complete Guide to Investing in High-Yield Stocks for Long-Term Financial Success and Growing Your Portfolio to Generate Passive Income

Lewis Finan

Table of Contents

Introduction

Welcome to "Dividend Stocks: A Complete Guide to Investing in High-Yield Stocks for Long-Term Financial Success and Growing Your Portfolio to Generate Passive Income." Whether you are a seasoned investor looking to enhance your strategy or a newcomer eager to learn about the benefits of dividend investing, this book aims to be your comprehensive resource for navigating the world of dividend stocks.

The Power of Dividend Investing

Dividend investing is a time-tested strategy that has helped countless investors build substantial wealth and achieve financial independence. Unlike growth stocks that primarily focus on capital appreciation, dividend stocks provide a steady stream of income through regular payouts, making them an attractive option for those seeking both income and growth.

Why Dividend Stocks?

Dividend stocks offer several compelling advantages:

- **Passive Income Generation**: One of the most appealing aspects of dividend stocks is their ability to generate passive income. This means you can earn money without actively working for it, providing a reliable source of income in various market conditions.

- **Compounding Returns**: By reinvesting your dividends, you can take advantage of the power of compounding. Over time, this can significantly increase your overall returns and help grow your portfolio faster.
- **Stability and Predictability**: Companies that consistently pay dividends tend to be more stable and financially healthy. This predictability can provide a sense of security, especially during volatile market periods.
- **Inflation Hedge**: Dividend payments often increase over time, helping to protect your purchasing power against inflation.

Overview of the Book

This book is structured to guide you through the entire process of dividend investing, from the basics to advanced strategies. Here's a brief overview of what you can expect in each chapter:

- **Chapter 1: Understanding Dividend Stocks** – We'll start with the fundamentals, explaining what dividend stocks are, why companies pay dividends, and the key terms you need to know.
- **Chapter 2: The Benefits of Dividend Investing** – This chapter will delve into the numerous advantages of dividend investing, including generating passive income, reinvesting dividends, and achieving compounding returns.
- **Chapter 3: How to Choose Dividend Stocks** – Learn how to evaluate and select the best dividend stocks based on yield, payout ratio, growth rate, and financial health.
- **Chapter 4: Strategies for Building a Dividend Portfolio** – Discover effective strategies for creating a diversified portfolio,

balancing high yield and growth, and considering international stocks and tax implications.

- **Chapter 5: Managing and Monitoring Your Dividend Portfolio** – Find out how to maintain your portfolio, analyze earnings reports, adjust for dividend changes, and use technology to stay on top of your investments.
- **Chapter 6: Advanced Dividend Investing Techniques** – Explore more sophisticated strategies, including investing in Dividend Aristocrats, high-yield stocks, REITs, and using options.
- **Chapter 7: Case Studies and Real-World Examples** – Gain insights from real-world examples and success stories, learn from common mistakes, and see how to build a sample portfolio.

In addition to these chapters, the book includes appendices with a glossary of terms, recommended resources, useful websites, and a dividend investing checklist to help you on your journey.

Your Journey to Financial Success

Dividend investing is more than just a strategy; it's a path to financial independence and long-term success. By following the principles and strategies outlined in this book, you can build a robust portfolio that not only provides a steady income but also grows your wealth over time.

We hope this book serves as a valuable guide and reference as you embark on your dividend investing journey. Whether you're aiming for financial security, supplementing your income, or achieving complete financial freedom, dividend stocks can play a crucial role in helping you reach your goals.

Happy investing!

Chapter 1: Understanding Dividend Stocks

Imagine this: you're sitting in a sunlit café, sipping on a perfectly brewed cup of coffee. Across from you, an old friend leans in, eager to share some exciting news about a recent investment that's been quietly growing their wealth. Their eyes sparkle with enthusiasm as they mention a term that might be new to you—dividend stocks.

Dividend stocks. The phrase itself might sound a bit dry, perhaps conjuring up images of Wall Street analysts in stuffy suits. But let's peel back the layers and dive into the world of dividend stocks, a world that is as vibrant and dynamic as any marketplace. This chapter will guide you through the essentials, painting a clear picture of what dividend stocks are, why they matter, and how they can play a pivotal role in your investment strategy.

What Are Dividend Stocks?

At its core, a dividend stock is a share in a company that regularly pays out a portion of its profits to shareholders. These payments, known as dividends, are typically made every quarter, though the schedule can vary. The key idea here is that companies reward their investors by distributing a slice of the earnings pie.

To understand this better, let's use an analogy. Picture a dividend stock as a tree in an orchard. You, the investor, own one or more of these trees. Throughout the year, the tree grows and thrives, absorbing sunlight and nutrients. When the season is right, the tree bears fruit. These fruits are your dividends—a tangible reward for owning the tree and nurturing its growth.

The Appeal of Dividend Stocks

Why are dividend stocks so appealing? There are several compelling reasons. First, they provide a source of regular income. This can be particularly attractive for retirees or anyone looking to supplement their income without selling off their investments.

For instance, consider Sarah, a retired teacher who invested in dividend stocks over the years. Each quarter, she receives dividend payments that help cover her living expenses. This steady stream of income gives her financial independence and peace of mind.

Second, dividend stocks can offer stability. Companies that pay dividends tend to be well-established with a history of profitability. These aren't the high-flying tech startups with volatile stock prices; rather, they are often mature businesses with predictable earnings. This can make them less risky than growth stocks, which are companies that reinvest earnings to fuel further growth rather than pay dividends.

Moreover, dividends can act as a buffer during market downturns. When stock prices fall, dividend payments can provide a cushion, reducing the overall impact on your portfolio. It's like having an umbrella during a sudden rainstorm—while others may scramble for cover, you remain relatively dry and secure.

How Dividends Work

Now, let's get into the mechanics of how dividends work. When a company earns a profit, its management team decides what portion of those profits should be reinvested in the business and what portion should be distributed to shareholders as dividends. This decision is influenced by various factors, including the company's growth prospects, current financial health, and strategic goals.

The amount paid out is usually expressed as a dividend per share. For example, if a company declares an annual dividend of $2 per share and you own 100 shares, you would receive $200 in dividends for that year. These payments can be taken as cash or, in some cases, reinvested to purchase more shares of the company, a process known as a dividend reinvestment plan (DRIP).

A key metric to understand here is the dividend yield, which is the annual dividend payment divided by the stock's current price. For instance, if a stock priced at $50 pays an annual dividend of $2, the dividend yield is 4%. This yield helps investors gauge the return they can expect from dividends alone, independent of any changes in the stock price.

Types of Dividend Stocks

Not all dividend stocks are created equal. They can broadly be categorized into several types, each with its unique characteristics and appeal.

- **Blue-Chip Stocks**: These are shares of large, well-established, and financially sound companies with a history of reliable performance. Examples include household names like Johnson & Johnson, Coca-Cola, and Procter & Gamble. Blue-chip stocks are known for their stability and consistent dividend payments.
- **Dividend Aristocrats**: This elite group consists of companies that have not only paid dividends but have also increased their dividend payouts annually for at least 25 consecutive years. Investing in

dividend aristocrats is like owning a finely tuned watch—precise, reliable, and steadily increasing in value.

- **Real Estate Investment Trusts (REITs)**: These are companies that own, operate, or finance income-producing real estate. REITs are required by law to distribute at least 90% of their taxable income to shareholders as dividends, making them a robust source of dividend income. They offer exposure to the real estate market without the need to directly own property.
- **Utility Stocks**: Companies in the utility sector—such as electric, gas, and water utilities—are known for paying high dividends. These companies typically have stable and predictable revenue streams, as they provide essential services that are always in demand.

Risks and Considerations

While dividend stocks can be a valuable addition to any portfolio, they are not without risks. It's essential to be aware of these before diving in.

- **Dividend Cuts**: Companies can reduce or eliminate dividend payments during tough economic times or if they need to conserve cash. This can negatively impact your income and the stock's price.
- **Interest Rate Sensitivity**: Dividend stocks can be sensitive to changes in interest rates. When interest rates rise, bonds and other fixed-income investments become more attractive, potentially leading to a decline in the price of dividend stocks.
- **Tax Considerations**: Dividend income is subject to taxes, which can vary based on your country's tax laws and the type of

dividends (qualified or non-qualified). It's crucial to understand the tax implications of your dividend investments.

Building a Dividend Stock Portfolio

Constructing a dividend stock portfolio involves careful selection and diversification. Aim to include a mix of different types of dividend stocks to spread risk. Consider factors such as dividend yield, payout ratio (the percentage of earnings paid as dividends), and the company's overall financial health.

For example, you might start with a few blue-chip stocks for stability, add some dividend aristocrats for growing income, include REITs for real estate exposure, and round out with utility stocks for high dividends. This diversified approach helps balance income generation with potential growth and risk management.

Dividend stocks offer a fascinating and potentially rewarding investment avenue. They provide regular income, offer stability, and can serve as a hedge against market volatility. By understanding how they work, recognizing their appeal, and being mindful of the associated risks, you can harness the power of dividend stocks to build a robust and resilient portfolio.

So, as you finish your coffee and part ways with your friend, consider taking a closer look at dividend stocks. They might just be the key to growing your wealth and securing a steady stream of income for years to come. Whether you're a seasoned investor or just starting, the world of dividend stocks is rich with opportunities waiting to be explored.

1.1 What Are Dividend Stocks?

Dividend stocks are shares in companies that distribute a portion of their earnings to shareholders in the form of dividends. These payments are typically made regularly—often quarterly—but the frequency can vary depending on the company's policy.

To understand dividend stocks more clearly, let's break down the key components:

1. Dividends Explained

Dividends are essentially a way for companies to share their profits with investors. When a company earns a profit, it can do several things with that money. It might reinvest in the business to foster growth, pay down debt, or hold onto the cash for future opportunities. Alternatively, it can distribute some of those profits to shareholders as dividends.

These dividends are usually paid in cash, directly into your brokerage account. However, some companies offer the option to receive dividends in the form of additional shares, known as stock dividends. This is part of a dividend reinvestment plan (DRIP), which allows investors to automatically reinvest their dividends to purchase more shares of the company.

2. Why Companies Pay Dividends

Not all companies pay dividends. Those that do are often well-established and financially stable. They might not have as many growth opportunities as younger companies, so they choose to reward shareholders with a portion of their profits instead.

For example, many companies in mature industries, such as utilities, consumer goods, and financial services, are known for their dividend payments. These companies have predictable revenue streams and less need for aggressive reinvestment, making them ideal candidates for regular dividend payments.

3. How Dividends Are Declared and Paid

Dividends are declared by a company's board of directors. When a dividend is declared, the company announces the amount of the dividend (e.g., $0.50 per share), the record date, and the payment date.

- **Record Date**: This is the date by which you must own the stock to be eligible to receive the dividend. If you purchase the stock after this date, you won't receive the upcoming dividend.
- **Payment Date**: This is the date on which the dividend will be paid to shareholders.

Let's use an example to illustrate this process:

Suppose Company XYZ announces a dividend of $1 per share with a record date of June 15th and a payment date of June 30th. If you own 100 shares of XYZ stock on or before June 15th, you will receive a $100 dividend on June 30th.

4. Dividend Yield and Payout Ratio

Two important metrics to understand when evaluating dividend stocks are the dividend yield and the payout ratio.

- **Dividend Yield**: This is calculated by dividing the annual dividend payment by the current stock price. For instance, if a stock is priced at $50 and pays an annual dividend of $2, the dividend yield is 4%. This metric helps investors understand the return they can expect from dividends alone.
- **Payout Ratio**: This is the percentage of earnings paid out as dividends. For example, if a company earns $10 per share and pays a $2 dividend, the payout ratio is 20%. A lower payout ratio might indicate that the company is retaining more earnings to reinvest in growth, while a higher payout ratio could suggest a commitment to returning profits to shareholders.

5. Types of Dividend Stocks

Dividend stocks come in various forms, each with unique characteristics:

- **Blue-Chip Stocks**: These are shares of large, established companies known for their financial stability and reliable dividend payments. Examples include companies like Johnson & Johnson and Coca-Cola.
- **Dividend Aristocrats**: These are companies that have not only paid dividends but have also increased their dividend payouts annually for at least 25 consecutive years. They are considered a safe bet for consistent dividend income.
- **Real Estate Investment Trusts (REITs)**: These are companies that own, operate, or finance income-producing real estate. By law, REITs must distribute at least 90% of their taxable income to shareholders, making them a good source of dividend income.
- **Utility Stocks**: Companies in the utility sector often have stable and predictable revenue streams, making them reliable dividend payers.

In summary, dividend stocks are a compelling option for investors looking for regular income and financial stability. By understanding the basics of what dividend stocks are and how they work, you can make more informed decisions and potentially benefit from this investment strategy.

1.2 Types of Dividends: Cash vs. Stock

When it comes to dividends, companies have a couple of primary options for rewarding their shareholders: cash dividends and stock dividends. Each type has its characteristics and implications for investors. Let's delve into the differences and benefits of each.

1. Cash Dividends

Cash dividends are the most common type of dividend. As the name suggests, these dividends are paid out in cash, usually deposited directly into the shareholder's brokerage account or sent via check. Here's a closer look at the key aspects of cash dividends:

How Cash Dividends Work

When a company declares a cash dividend, it specifies an amount per share. For instance, if a company declares a $1 per share dividend and you own 100 shares, you will receive $100. The company sets a record date and a payment date for these dividends.

- **Record Date**: The cutoff date by which you must be a registered shareholder to receive the dividend.
- **Payment Date**: The date on which the dividend will be paid out to shareholders.

Benefits of Cash Dividends

- **Immediate Income**: Cash dividends provide shareholders with immediate income, which can be particularly beneficial for retirees or those seeking regular cash flow.
- **Flexibility**: Investors can use the cash dividends as they see fit—whether for reinvestment, covering living expenses, or other financial goals.

- **Certainty**: Cash dividends offer a clear and straightforward return on investment, making them appealing to conservative investors.

Considerations for Cash Dividends

- **Taxation**: Cash dividends are typically subject to taxes. The tax rate can depend on whether the dividends are qualified or non-qualified, as well as the investor's tax bracket.
- **Reinvestment**: If you choose to reinvest cash dividends to buy more shares, there might be transaction fees unless you're using a dividend reinvestment plan (DRIP).

2. Stock Dividends

Stock dividends, also known as bonus shares, are paid out in the form of additional shares of the company's stock. Instead of receiving cash, shareholders receive more shares based on the number of shares they already own.

How Stock Dividends Work

When a company declares a stock dividend, it specifies the rate, such as a 5% stock dividend. If you own 100 shares and a 5% stock dividend is declared, you will receive 5 additional shares, bringing your total to 105 shares.

Benefits of Stock Dividends

- **Growth Potential**: Receiving additional shares increases your stake in the company, potentially leading to greater capital appreciation over time.
- **Tax Deferral**: In many cases, stock dividends are not taxed until the shares are sold, allowing for tax deferral.
- **Compounding**: Stock dividends can accelerate the compounding effect in your investment portfolio, especially if the company continues to perform well.

Considerations for Stock Dividends

- **Dilution**: Issuing additional shares can dilute the value of existing shares, as the company's earnings are spread over a larger number of shares.
- **Market Impact**: Sometimes, the market may perceive stock dividends as a sign that the company prefers to conserve cash, which can impact the stock price.
- **Less Immediate Liquidity**: Unlike cash dividends, stock dividends do not provide immediate liquidity. Investors looking for regular income might prefer cash dividends.

Choosing Between Cash and Stock Dividends

The choice between cash and stock dividends often depends on an investor's financial goals, tax situation, and market outlook. Here are a few scenarios to consider:

- **Income Needs**: If you rely on your investments for regular income, cash dividends are likely more suitable. They provide a steady stream of income that can be used immediately.
- **Long-Term Growth**: If you're focused on long-term growth and are comfortable with the potential for market fluctuations, stock dividends might be a better option. They allow you to increase your holdings in the company without additional cash outlay.
- **Tax Strategy**: Consider the tax implications of both types of dividends. In some cases, reinvesting cash dividends through a DRIP might offer a middle ground, combining the benefits of both approaches.

Understanding the differences between cash and stock dividends is crucial for making informed investment decisions. Cash dividends provide immediate income and flexibility, making them ideal for income-focused investors. Stock dividends, on the other hand, offer growth potential and tax advantages, appealing to those with a long-term investment horizon. By aligning your dividend preferences with your financial goals, you can optimize your investment strategy and enhance your overall portfolio performance.

1.3 Why Companies Pay Dividends

When companies decide to pay dividends, they are making a strategic choice about how to use their profits. This decision is influenced by various factors, including the company's financial health, growth prospects, and shareholder expectations. Let's explore the primary reasons why companies choose to pay dividends and what this means for investors.

1. Signaling Financial Health

One of the main reasons companies pay dividends is to signal their financial stability and strength. Dividends can be a sign that a company is generating sufficient profits and cash flow, which allows it to reward shareholders while still reinvesting in the business.

Confidence in Future Earnings

When a company consistently pays dividends, it demonstrates confidence in its future earnings potential. Investors often view dividend payments as a sign that management believes the company will continue to perform well, providing a steady source of income.

Attracting and Retaining Investors

Dividend payments can also help attract and retain investors, particularly those seeking regular income. Many income-focused investors, such as retirees and institutional investors, prioritize companies that pay reliable dividends. By offering dividends, companies can broaden their investor base and potentially enhance stock price stability.

2. Rewarding Shareholders

Paying dividends is a direct way for companies to reward their shareholders. When investors purchase shares, they are essentially buying a piece of the company and its future profits. Dividends are a tangible return on this investment, providing a regular income stream.

Providing Income

Dividends offer a steady income stream, which can be particularly important for certain investors. For example, retirees often rely on dividend income to cover living expenses. By paying dividends, companies can provide a reliable source of income that enhances investor loyalty.

Enhancing Shareholder Value

In addition to providing income, dividends can enhance overall shareholder value. When companies pay dividends, they reduce the risk of misallocation of profits. Instead of holding excessive cash, which might be spent inefficiently, they return funds to shareholders who can reinvest them as they see fit.

3. Reflecting Mature Business Stage

Many companies that pay dividends are in a mature stage of their business lifecycle. These companies often have stable revenue streams and fewer growth opportunities compared to younger, more aggressive firms. As a result, they might not need to reinvest all their profits back into the business.

Limited Reinvestment Opportunities

For mature companies with limited opportunities for reinvestment, paying dividends is a way to make efficient use of their earnings. Instead of hoarding cash or making unwise investments, they distribute profits to shareholders, who can then decide how to best use those funds.

Balancing Growth and Income

Even mature companies can balance growth and income. They might allocate a portion of their profits to dividends while still investing in strategic projects. This approach allows them to reward shareholders and pursue growth opportunities simultaneously.

4. Maintaining Investor Confidence

Paying consistent dividends can help maintain investor confidence, particularly during economic downturns or periods of market volatility. Regular dividend payments can reassure investors that the company remains financially sound and committed to returning value to shareholders.

Stability in Uncertain Times

During uncertain times, dividends can provide a sense of stability. Even if a company's stock price fluctuates, the continuity of dividend payments can offer a reliable return, mitigating some of the anxiety associated with market volatility.

Reinforcing Trust

By maintaining or even increasing dividend payments during challenging periods, companies can reinforce trust among their investors. This commitment to shareholder returns can build long-term loyalty and support the stock price.

5. Competitive Advantage

In some industries, paying dividends can provide a competitive advantage. Companies known for their reliable dividend payments may attract more investors, which can lead to higher stock valuations and greater financial flexibility.

Differentiation

Dividends can differentiate a company from its competitors. In sectors where few companies pay dividends, those that do can stand out as more investor-friendly, potentially attracting a dedicated following of income-seeking investors.

Financial Discipline

Regular dividend payments impose a level of financial discipline on a company. Management must ensure that sufficient cash is available to meet dividend commitments, which can encourage prudent financial management and efficient capital allocation.

Companies pay dividends for a variety of reasons, ranging from signaling financial health and rewarding shareholders to maintaining investor confidence and gaining a competitive edge. For investors, understanding these motivations is crucial for making informed investment decisions. By choosing companies with a solid dividend policy, investors can benefit from regular income, potential stock price stability, and overall enhanced shareholder value. As you consider adding dividend stocks to your portfolio, keep these factors in mind to align your investments with your financial goals and risk tolerance.

1.4 Key Terms and Concepts

When exploring the world of dividend stocks, it's essential to understand some key terms and concepts. These will help you navigate investment strategies, evaluate potential stocks, and make informed decisions. Let's break down the most important ones.

1. Dividend

A dividend is a portion of a company's earnings that is paid out to shareholders. Dividends are typically distributed in cash, but they can also be issued as additional shares of stock.

2. Dividend Yield

The dividend yield is a financial ratio that shows how much a company pays out in dividends each year relative to its stock price. It is calculated by dividing the annual dividend per share by the stock's current price per share.

$$\text{Dividend Yield} = \frac{\text{Annual Dividend per Share}}{\text{Price per Share}}$$

For example, if a company's stock is priced at $50 and it pays an annual dividend of $2, the dividend yield is 4%.

3. Payout Ratio

The payout ratio is the percentage of a company's earnings that are paid out as dividends. It is calculated by dividing the total dividends paid by the net income of the company.

$$\text{Payout Ratio} = \frac{\text{Dividends Paid}}{\text{Net Income}}$$

A payout ratio of 50% means the company is returning half of its earnings to shareholders as dividends and retaining the other half for reinvestment.

4. Ex-Dividend Date

The ex-dividend date is the cutoff date to be eligible to receive the next dividend payment. If you purchase a stock on or after the ex-dividend date, you will not receive the upcoming dividend.

5. Record Date

The record date is the date set by the company to determine which shareholders are eligible to receive the declared dividend. You must be on the company's books as a shareholder on this date to receive the dividend.

6. Payment Date

The payment date is the date on which the dividend will be paid out to shareholders. This is the day you will receive the dividend payment in your account.

7. Dividend Reinvestment Plan (DRIP)

A Dividend Reinvestment Plan (DRIP) is a program that allows shareholders to automatically reinvest their cash dividends to purchase additional shares of the company's stock, often without paying a commission.

8. Qualified vs. Non-Qualified Dividends

Qualified Dividends: These dividends meet specific IRS criteria and are taxed at the lower long-term capital gains tax rate.

Non-Qualified Dividends: These dividends do not meet the criteria for qualified dividends and are taxed at the higher ordinary income tax rate.

9. Dividend Growth Rate

The dividend growth rate is the annualized percentage rate of growth of a company's dividend payments. It indicates how much a company's dividend payments have increased over time.

10. Yield on Cost

Yield on cost is a measure of dividend yield based on the original purchase price of the stock. It is calculated by dividing the annual dividend by the original purchase price of the stock.

$$\text{Yield on Cost} = \frac{\text{Annual Dividend per Share}}{\text{Original Purchase Price}}$$

This metric can be particularly useful for long-term investors to assess how their dividend yield has improved over time.

Understanding these key terms and concepts is crucial for any investor looking to delve into dividend stocks. They provide the foundational knowledge necessary to evaluate potential investments, understand their income potential, and manage a dividend-focused portfolio effectively. With these concepts in your toolkit, you'll be better equipped to make informed decisions and optimize your investment strategy for both income and growth.

Chapter 2: The Benefits of Dividend Investing

In the world of investing, dividend stocks stand out for their unique set of advantages. In this chapter, we'll explore the numerous benefits of dividend investing and why it's an attractive strategy for investors seeking both income and long-term growth.

1. Reliable Income Stream

One of the primary benefits of dividend investing is the ability to generate a reliable income stream. Unlike bonds or other fixed-income investments, which typically pay interest at fixed intervals, dividends from well-established companies can provide a steady source of income regardless of market conditions. This income can be particularly valuable for retirees or anyone looking to supplement their earnings without having to sell off assets.

2. Potential for Growth

While dividends offer immediate income, dividend investing also provides the potential for long-term growth. Companies that pay dividends tend to be financially stable and mature, with a track record of consistent earnings. By reinvesting dividends back into additional shares of stock, investors can compound their returns over time, potentially accelerating wealth accumulation.

3. Historically Strong Performance

Historically, dividend-paying stocks have delivered strong performance compared to non-dividend-paying stocks. Studies have shown that dividend-paying companies tend to outperform the broader market over the long term, providing investors with both income and capital appreciation. This makes dividend investing an attractive option for those seeking to build wealth steadily over time.

4. Inflation Hedge

Dividend stocks also serve as a hedge against inflation. Unlike fixed-income investments, which may lose purchasing power over time as inflation erodes the value of future cash flows, dividends have the potential to grow over time, helping investors maintain their standard of living in an inflationary environment. Many companies increase their dividends regularly, providing investors with a built-in inflation hedge.

5. Lower Volatility

Dividend-paying stocks tend to exhibit lower volatility compared to non-dividend-paying stocks. This is because dividends provide a buffer during market downturns, helping to stabilize the stock price. Even if the market experiences a temporary decline, investors can still benefit from the regular income provided by dividends, reducing the overall impact on their investment portfolios.

6. Tax Advantages

Dividend income is often taxed at a lower rate than interest income or capital gains, making dividend investing tax-efficient for many investors. Qualified dividends, which meet specific IRS criteria, are taxed at the long-term capital gains rate, which is typically lower than the ordinary income tax rate. This can result in significant tax savings, especially for investors in higher tax brackets.

In conclusion, dividend investing offers a host of benefits that make it an attractive strategy for investors of all backgrounds and risk tolerances. From providing a reliable income stream and potential for growth to serving as an inflation hedge and offering tax advantages, dividend stocks have much to offer. By incorporating dividend-paying stocks into a well-diversified investment portfolio, investors can benefit from both income and long-term capital appreciation, helping them achieve their financial goals over time.

2.1 Passive Income Generation

In the vast landscape of investing, few strategies offer the allure of passive income generation quite like dividend investing. It's a concept that resonates deeply with investors seeking financial independence, wealth accumulation, and a steady stream of income without the demands of active management. In this chapter, we'll delve deep into the intricacies of passive income generation through dividend investing, exploring its mechanisms, benefits, and strategies for success.

Understanding Passive Income and Dividend Investing

Passive income is income earned with minimal effort or active involvement. It's the holy grail for many investors—a source of wealth that continues to flow even when they're not actively working. Dividend investing, specifically, is a cornerstone of passive income generation. When you invest in dividend-paying stocks, you become a part-owner of the company, entitled to a share of its profits. These profits are distributed to shareholders in the form of dividends, providing a steady income stream.

The Mechanics of Dividend Income

Dividend income operates on a simple premise: companies share a portion of their profits with their shareholders. This distribution typically occurs regularly—quarterly, in most cases—but can vary depending on the company's dividend policy. As a shareholder, you receive these dividend payments without having to actively manage the investment. It's a passive income stream that requires little to no effort on your part, making it an attractive option for those seeking financial freedom.

Benefits of Passive Income from Dividend Stocks

1. **Steady Stream of Income**: Dividend stocks offer a reliable stream of income, making them particularly appealing for retirees or anyone seeking to supplement their earnings. Unlike other investment vehicles that rely on capital appreciation, dividend

income provides a consistent cash flow, regardless of market fluctuations.

2. **Financial Independence**: Passive income from dividend stocks can contribute to financial independence by reducing reliance on active income sources. By building a portfolio of dividend-paying stocks, investors can create a source of passive income that grows over time, providing greater financial security and peace of mind.

3. **Flexibility**: Dividend income offers flexibility in how it can be used. Investors can choose to reinvest dividends to purchase additional shares of stock, further compounding their returns, or use the income to cover living expenses, travel, or other financial goals. This flexibility allows investors to tailor their investment strategy to their individual needs and objectives.

4. **Diversification**: Dividend investing allows for diversification across different sectors, industries, and geographic regions. By investing in a variety of dividend-paying companies, investors can spread risk and reduce the impact of market fluctuations on their overall income. Diversification is a key principle of sound investing and can help mitigate potential losses while maximizing returns.

Strategies for Success in Dividend Investing

While dividend investing offers numerous benefits, success requires careful planning and execution. Here are some strategies to consider:

1. **Focus on Quality**: When selecting dividend stocks, prioritize companies with a track record of stable earnings, strong cash flow, and a history of consistent dividend payments. Look for companies

with a competitive advantage, strong management team, and a sustainable business model.

2. **Dividend Growth**: Seek out companies with a history of increasing their dividends over time. These companies demonstrate financial strength and a commitment to returning value to shareholders. Dividend growth stocks can provide both income and capital appreciation, making them a valuable addition to any portfolio.

3. **Reinvestment**: Consider reinvesting dividends to purchase additional shares of stock through a dividend reinvestment plan (DRIP). Reinvesting dividends allows for compounding returns over time, accelerating wealth accumulation and income growth.

4. **Diversification**: Diversify your dividend portfolio across different sectors, industries, and geographic regions to spread risk and maximize returns. Avoid overconcentration in any single stock or sector, as this can increase the volatility of your portfolio.

5. **Long-Term Perspective**: Approach dividend investing with a long-term perspective. Focus on building a portfolio of high-quality dividend stocks that can provide steady income and growth over time. Resist the temptation to chase short-term gains or react impulsively to market fluctuations.

Passive income generation through dividend investing is a powerful wealth-building strategy that offers investors a reliable source of income with minimal effort. By investing in dividend-paying stocks, individuals can build a portfolio that generates passive income over time, providing financial independence, flexibility, and peace of mind. Whether you're a seasoned investor or just starting, dividend investing offers a compelling opportunity to build wealth and achieve your financial goals. With careful planning, disciplined investing, and a long-term perspective, dividend stocks can pave the way to a brighter financial future.

2.2 Dividend Reinvestment Plans (DRIPs)

Dividend Reinvestment Plans, commonly referred to as DRIPs, are powerful tools that allow investors to harness the benefits of compounding returns and automate the reinvestment of dividends. In this chapter, we'll explore the ins and outs of DRIPs, including how they work, their benefits, and considerations for investors looking to leverage this strategy.

Understanding Dividend Reinvestment Plans (DRIPs)

DRIPs are investment programs offered by companies that allow shareholders to reinvest their cash dividends to purchase additional shares of stock directly from the company. Instead of receiving dividend payments in cash, investors can opt to have these dividends automatically reinvested to acquire more shares of the same company's stock.

How DRIPs Work

When you enroll in a DRIP, the dividends you earn from your shares of stock are automatically used to purchase additional shares of the same stock. These additional shares are typically purchased at the market price on the dividend payment date, often without incurring any transaction fees. Over time, the number of shares in your investment portfolio grows, leading to increased dividend payments in the future.

Benefits of DRIPs

1. **Compounding Returns**: DRIPs harness the power of compounding returns by reinvesting dividends to purchase additional shares of stock. Over time, this compounding effect can significantly increase the size of your investment portfolio and boost long-term returns.
2. **Automatic and Convenient**: DRIPs offer investors a convenient way to reinvest dividends without having to take any action. Once enrolled, dividends are automatically reinvested, allowing for seamless and hassle-free wealth accumulation.
3. **Cost-Effective**: Many DRIPs allow investors to purchase additional shares of stock without incurring any transaction fees. This can result in significant cost savings over time, especially for investors looking to regularly reinvest dividends.
4. **Dollar-Cost Averaging**: By reinvesting dividends at regular intervals, DRIPs facilitate dollar-cost averaging, a strategy that involves investing a fixed amount of money at predetermined intervals. Dollar-cost averaging can help smooth out the impact of market fluctuations and reduce the risk of investing a large sum of money at the wrong time.
5. **Long-Term Growth**: DRIPs are well-suited for long-term investors looking to build wealth steadily over time. By reinvesting dividends to purchase additional shares of stock, investors can take advantage of compounding returns and benefit from the growth potential of dividend-paying companies.

Considerations for Investors

While DRIPs offer numerous benefits, there are some considerations for investors to keep in mind:

1. **Tax Implications**: Reinvested dividends are still subject to taxation, even though they are not received in cash. Investors should be aware of the tax implications of DRIPs and consult with a tax advisor if necessary.
2. **Lack of Flexibility**: DRIPs may limit investors' ability to use dividend income for other purposes, such as covering living expenses or making other investments. Investors should carefully consider their financial goals and liquidity needs before enrolling in a DRIP.
3. **Company-Specific Risks**: DRIPs are offered by individual companies, which means investors are exposed to company-specific risks. Before enrolling in a DRIP, investors should conduct thorough research on the company's financial health, business model, and dividend history.

Dividend Reinvestment Plans (DRIPs) offer investors a powerful tool for harnessing the benefits of compounding returns and automating the reinvestment of dividends. By enrolling in a DRIP, investors can take advantage of compounding growth, cost-effective investing, and the convenience of automatic reinvestment. While DRIPs may not be suitable for every investor, they can be a valuable addition to a long-term investment strategy, helping investors build wealth steadily over time. With careful consideration of the benefits and risks, investors can leverage DRIPs to achieve their financial goals and create a path to long-term financial success.

2.3 Compounding Returns over Time

Compounding returns is a powerful concept in investing that allows investors to grow their wealth exponentially over time. In this chapter, we'll explore how compounding works, its impact on investment returns, and strategies for maximizing its benefits.

Understanding Compounding Returns

Compounding is the process by which an investment earns returns on both the principal amount and the accumulated earnings from previous periods. In other words, as your investment generates returns, those returns are reinvested to generate additional earnings, leading to exponential growth over time.

How Compounding Works

The key to compounding is time. The longer your investment remains invested, the more time it has to grow and compound. Even small returns can have a significant impact over time when allowed to compound over many years or decades.

For example, let's say you invest $1,000 in a dividend-paying stock with an average annual return of 8%. After the first year, your investment would grow to $1,080. In the second year, you would earn returns not only on your initial $1,000 investment but also on the $80 in earnings from the first year. Over time, this compounding effect can result in substantial wealth accumulation.

Benefits of Compounding Returns

1. **Exponential Growth**: Compounding returns allow investments to grow exponentially over time. The longer your money remains invested, the greater the growth potential.
2. **Passive Wealth Accumulation**: Once set in motion, compounding requires minimal effort on the part of the investor. By reinvesting earnings and allowing them to compound, investors can passively accumulate wealth over time.
3. **Risk Mitigation**: Compounding returns can help mitigate the impact of market volatility and fluctuations. By reinvesting earnings during downturns, investors can take advantage of lower prices and position themselves for future growth.
4. **Long-Term Financial Goals**: Compounding returns are particularly well-suited for achieving long-term financial goals, such as retirement savings or wealth preservation. By starting early and allowing investments to compound over several decades, investors can build a substantial nest egg for the future.

Strategies for Maximizing Compounding Returns

1. **Start Early**: The most effective way to maximize compounding returns is to start investing early. The earlier you begin investing, the more time your money has to compound and grow.
2. **Stay Invested**: Consistency is key to maximizing compounding returns. Avoid trying to time the market or make frequent changes to your investment portfolio. Instead, stay invested for the long term and allow your investments to compound over time.
3. **Reinvest Dividends**: Reinvesting dividends is a powerful way to accelerate compounding returns. By reinvesting dividends to

purchase additional shares of stock, investors can take advantage of the compounding effect and boost long-term growth.

4. **Diversify Your Portfolio**: Diversification can help reduce risk and maximize the potential for compounding returns. By spreading investments across different asset classes, sectors, and geographic regions, investors can capture opportunities for growth while mitigating the impact of market fluctuations.

Compounding returns over time is a fundamental principle of investing that allows investors to build wealth steadily and passively. By reinvesting earnings and allowing them to compound over many years or decades, investors can achieve exponential growth and reach their long-term financial goals. Whether you're just starting or are a seasoned investor, understanding the power of compounding returns can help you make informed decisions and create a path to financial success. With patience, discipline, and a long-term perspective, compounding returns can pave the way to a brighter financial future.

2.4 Stability and Predictability

In the realm of investing, stability, and predictability are highly sought-after qualities. Investors crave assurance that their investments will weather market volatility and deliver consistent returns over time. In this chapter, we'll explore how certain investment strategies, such as dividend investing, offer stability and predictability, providing investors with confidence and peace of mind.

Stability in Dividend Investing

Dividend investing is renowned for its stability, thanks to the predictable nature of dividend payments. Companies that pay dividends typically have established revenue streams, strong cash flow, and a history of consistent earnings. As a result, they are better equipped to weather economic downturns and market fluctuations, providing investors with a stable source of income regardless of prevailing market conditions.

Predictability of Dividend Payments

One of the key attractions of dividend investing is the predictability of dividend payments. Unlike capital gains, which are uncertain and dependent on market performance, dividends are typically paid out regularly—often quarterly—and are relatively stable over time. This predictability allows investors to plan and budget with confidence, knowing they can rely on a steady stream of income from their dividend investments.

Benefits of Stability and Predictability

1. **Income Stability**: Dividend investing offers investors a reliable source of income that is less susceptible to market volatility. By focusing on companies with a history of consistent dividend payments, investors can create a stable income stream to cover living expenses, retirement needs, or other financial goals.
2. **Portfolio Stability**: Dividend-paying stocks tend to exhibit lower volatility compared to non-dividend-paying stocks. This stability

can help cushion the impact of market downturns and provide investors with greater confidence in their investment portfolios, reducing the temptation to make impulsive decisions during periods of market turbulence.

3. **Long-Term Growth**: Stability and predictability are not mutually exclusive from growth. Dividend-paying stocks often offer the potential for long-term capital appreciation in addition to regular income. By reinvesting dividends and allowing them to compound over time, investors can achieve both stability and growth in their investment portfolios.

4. **Risk Mitigation**: Stable, dividend-paying companies are often less risky investments compared to high-growth, speculative stocks. Their established business models, consistent earnings, and reliable dividend payments help mitigate the risk of capital loss, providing investors with greater peace of mind and security.

Stability and predictability are invaluable qualities in investing, offering investors assurance and confidence in their financial future. Dividend investing exemplifies these qualities, providing investors with a stable source of income and predictable returns over time. By focusing on companies with a history of consistent dividend payments, investors can build a resilient investment portfolio that withstands market volatility and delivers long-term growth. With stability and predictability as guiding principles, investors can navigate the complexities of the market with greater clarity and conviction, ultimately achieving their financial goals with confidence and peace of mind.

Chapter 3: How to Choose Dividend Stocks

Selecting the right dividend stocks is crucial for investors seeking to build a portfolio that generates consistent income and long-term growth. In this chapter, we'll explore the key factors to consider when choosing dividend stocks, from assessing dividend metrics to evaluating the financial health of companies.

1. Understanding Dividend Metrics

Before diving into specific stocks, it's essential to understand the key dividend metrics that investors use to evaluate potential investments. These metrics provide valuable insights into a company's dividend-paying ability and sustainability.

Dividend Yield

The dividend yield is a measure of a company's annual dividend payments relative to its stock price. It is calculated by dividing the annual dividend per share by the current stock price. A higher dividend yield indicates a higher percentage return on investment from dividends.

Payout Ratio

The payout ratio is the proportion of a company's earnings that are paid out as dividends to shareholders. It is calculated by dividing the total dividends paid by the net income of the company. A lower payout ratio suggests that a company has more room to increase its dividends in the future.

Dividend Growth Rate

The dividend growth rate measures the annualized rate at which a company's dividends have increased over time. It provides insights into the company's commitment to returning value to shareholders and its ability to sustain and grow dividends in the future.

2. Evaluating Company Fundamentals

In addition to dividend metrics, it's essential to evaluate the overall financial health and stability of the companies you're considering for investment. Here are some key factors to consider:

Revenue and Earnings Growth

Look for companies with a history of stable revenue and earnings growth. Companies with consistent growth are more likely to sustain and grow their dividend payments over time.

Debt Levels

Assess the company's debt levels and debt-to-equity ratio. Companies with high debt levels may be less able to maintain their dividend payments during economic downturns or periods of financial stress.

Cash Flow

Evaluate the company's cash flow to ensure it has sufficient funds to cover dividend payments. A strong and consistent cash flow is essential for supporting dividend payments, especially during challenging economic conditions.

Industry and Market Position

Consider the company's industry and market position. Companies operating in stable and growing industries are more likely to maintain and grow their dividend payments over time.

3. Diversification and Risk Management

Diversification is key to building a resilient dividend portfolio that can weather market volatility and economic uncertainties. Spread your investments across different sectors, industries, and geographic regions to reduce risk and maximize potential returns.

Choosing dividend stocks requires careful consideration of a variety of factors, from dividend metrics and company fundamentals to diversification and risk management. By focusing on companies with strong financial health, sustainable dividend payments, and a commitment to shareholder value, investors can build a portfolio that generates consistent income and long-term growth. With thorough research and disciplined investing, dividend stocks can play a crucial role in achieving your financial goals and securing your financial future.

3.1 Evaluating Dividend Yield

Dividend yield is a critical metric for investors seeking to assess the income potential of dividend-paying stocks. It provides valuable insights into the relationship between a company's dividend payments and its stock price, helping investors identify attractive investment opportunities. Here's how to evaluate dividend yield effectively:

Understanding Dividend Yield

The dividend yield is calculated by dividing the annual dividend per share by the current stock price and expressing the result as a percentage. Mathematically, it is represented as:

$$\text{Dividend Yield} = \frac{\text{Annual Dividend per Share}}{\text{Stock Price}} \times 100\%$$

For example, if a company pays an annual dividend of $2 per share and its stock price is $50 per share, the dividend yield would be 4%:

$$\text{Dividend Yield} = \frac{\$2}{\$50} \times 100\% = 4\%$$

Interpreting Dividend Yield

- **High Dividend Yield**: A high dividend yield relative to the stock price indicates that the company is distributing a significant portion of its earnings to shareholders. While a high dividend yield can be attractive for income-oriented investors, it may also signal that the stock price has declined, potentially due to underlying issues with the company's financial health or future growth prospects.

- **Low Dividend Yield**: Conversely, a low dividend yield relative to the stock price may indicate that the company is retaining more of its earnings for reinvestment in growth opportunities. While a low dividend yield may disappoint income-oriented investors, it can also signal confidence from management in the company's ability to generate future growth and increase dividends over time.

Factors to Consider

When evaluating dividend yield, it's essential to consider the following factors:

- **Historical Dividend Yield**: Assess the company's historical dividend yield and compare it to current levels. A consistent or increasing dividend yield over time may indicate a commitment to returning value to shareholders.
- **Dividend Sustainability**: Evaluate the sustainability of the company's dividend payments by assessing its payout ratio, cash flow, and earnings growth. A high payout ratio or declining earnings could signal potential risks to the sustainability of dividend payments.
- **Industry and Market Conditions**: Consider industry and market conditions when evaluating dividend yield. Companies operating in stable and mature industries may offer higher dividend yields, while those in growth-oriented sectors may prioritize reinvestment in future growth opportunities over dividend payments.
- **Total Return Perspective**: Remember to consider dividend yield in conjunction with other investment metrics, such as capital

appreciation potential and total return. A stock with a lower dividend yield but strong growth prospects may offer greater total return potential over the long term.

Evaluating dividend yield is a crucial step in identifying attractive dividend-paying stocks for investment. By understanding the relationship between dividend payments and stock price and considering factors such as historical performance, dividend sustainability, and industry dynamics, investors can make informed decisions that align with their investment objectives and risk tolerance. With thorough research and careful analysis, dividend yield can serve as a valuable tool for building a diversified portfolio that generates consistent income and long-term growth.

3.2 Dividend Payout Ratio

The dividend payout ratio is a fundamental metric used by investors to evaluate the sustainability of a company's dividend payments. It provides insights into the proportion of a company's earnings that are distributed to shareholders as dividends, helping investors assess the company's ability to maintain and grow its dividend payments over time. Here's how to understand and interpret the dividend payout ratio effectively:

Understanding the Dividend Payout Ratio

The dividend payout ratio is calculated by dividing the total dividends paid by the company by its net income and expressing the result as a percentage. Mathematically, it is represented as:

$$\text{Dividend Payout Ratio} = \frac{\text{Dividends Paid}}{\text{Net Income}} \times 100\%$$

For example, if a company pays out $1 million in dividends and has a net income of $5 million, the dividend payout ratio would be 20%:

$$\text{Dividend Payout Ratio} = \frac{\$1,000,000}{\$5,000,000} \times 100\% = 20\%$$

Interpreting Dividend Payout Ratio

Low Payout Ratio: A low dividend payout ratio suggests that the company is retaining a significant portion of its earnings for reinvestment in growth opportunities or to strengthen its financial position. While a low payout ratio may disappoint income-oriented investors seeking higher dividend payments, it can also indicate that the company has the flexibility to increase dividends in the future.

High Payout Ratio: Conversely, a high dividend payout ratio may indicate that the company is distributing a large portion of its earnings to shareholders as dividends. While a high payout ratio may be attractive for income-oriented investors in the short term, it could also signal that the company is not reinvesting sufficient earnings in growth opportunities or may have limited financial flexibility to weather economic downturns or unexpected expenses.

Factors to Consider

When evaluating the dividend payout ratio, it's essential to consider the following factors:

- **Industry Norms**: Compare the company's dividend payout ratio to industry norms and peers to assess its relative dividend policy and sustainability. Companies operating in different sectors may have varying payout ratios due to differences in business models, growth prospects, and capital allocation priorities.
- **Historical Trends**: Analyze the company's historical dividend payout ratio and trends over time. A consistent or declining payout ratio may indicate a stable dividend policy and disciplined capital allocation strategy.
- **Earnings Growth**: Consider the company's earnings growth prospects and trajectory when evaluating the dividend payout ratio. A company with strong earnings growth may have the capacity to sustain or increase its dividend payments over time, even with a moderate to high payout ratio.
- **Dividend Sustainability**: Assess the sustainability of the company's dividend payments by examining its cash flow, balance sheet strength, and dividend coverage ratio. A company with sufficient cash flow and financial stability is better positioned to maintain its dividend payments, even during challenging economic conditions.

The dividend payout ratio is a valuable metric for investors seeking to evaluate the sustainability and growth potential of dividend payments. By understanding and interpreting the dividend payout ratio in the context of industry norms, historical trends, earnings growth prospects, and dividend sustainability, investors can make informed decisions that align with their investment objectives and risk tolerance. With thorough research and careful analysis, the dividend payout ratio can serve as a valuable tool for identifying high-quality dividend-paying stocks for long-term investment success.

3.3 Dividend Growth Rate

The dividend growth rate is a crucial metric for investors evaluating the long-term potential of dividend-paying stocks. It measures the annualized rate at which a company's dividends have increased over a specified period, providing insights into the company's commitment to returning value to shareholders and its ability to sustain and grow dividends in the future. Here's how to understand and interpret the dividend growth rate effectively:

Understanding Dividend Growth Rate

The dividend growth rate is calculated by comparing the dividends paid by a company in two consecutive periods and expressing the percentage increase over that time frame. Mathematically, it is represented as:

$$\text{Dividend Growth Rate} = \frac{\text{Dividend in Current Period} - \text{Dividend in Previous Period}}{\text{Dividend in Previous Period}} \times 100\%$$

For example, if a company paid a dividend of $1 per share last year and increased it to $1.10 per share this year, the dividend growth rate would be 10%:

$$\text{Dividend Growth Rate} = \frac{\$1.10 - \$1.00}{\$1.00} \times 100\% = 10\%$$

Interpreting Dividend Growth Rate

- **Consistent Growth**: A consistent and increasing dividend growth rate indicates that the company is actively returning value to shareholders and has the financial strength to support dividend increases over time. Companies with a history of consistent dividend growth are often viewed favorably by income-oriented investors seeking reliable income streams and long-term capital appreciation.
- **Accelerating Growth**: Accelerating dividend growth may signal improving business fundamentals and earnings prospects. Companies that experience accelerating dividend growth may attract investors seeking higher income potential and capital appreciation as a result of improved financial performance and market conditions.

Factors to Consider

When evaluating the dividend growth rate, it's essential to consider the following factors:

- **Historical Trends**: Analyze the company's historical dividend growth rate and trends over time. A consistent or increasing dividend growth rate may indicate a commitment to returning value to shareholders and a disciplined capital allocation strategy.

- **Earnings Growth**: Assess the company's earnings growth prospects and trajectory when evaluating the dividend growth rate. Companies with strong and sustainable earnings growth are more likely to sustain and increase dividend payments over time, providing investors with a reliable income stream and potential for capital appreciation.
- **Dividend Sustainability**: Consider the sustainability of the company's dividend payments by examining its payout ratio, cash flow, and balance sheet strength. A company with sufficient cash flow and financial stability is better positioned to maintain and grow dividends, even during challenging economic conditions.
- **Industry Dynamics**: Evaluate industry dynamics and market conditions when assessing the dividend growth rate. Companies operating in stable and growing industries may have higher dividend growth rates, while those in cyclical or declining industries may experience slower growth or periodic dividend cuts.

The dividend growth rate is a critical metric for investors seeking to identify high-quality dividend-paying stocks with long-term income and growth potential. By understanding and interpreting the dividend growth rate in the context of historical trends, earnings growth prospects, dividend sustainability, and industry dynamics, investors can make informed decisions that align with their investment objectives and risk tolerance. With thorough research and careful analysis, the dividend growth rate can serve as a valuable tool for building a diversified portfolio that generates consistent income and long-term wealth accumulation.

3.4 Financial Health of a Company

Assessing the financial health of a company is essential for investors considering dividend-paying stocks. A company's financial strength and stability play a crucial role in its ability to maintain and grow dividend payments over time. Here's how to evaluate the financial health of a company effectively:

Understanding Financial Health Metrics

- **Revenue and Earnings Growth**: Evaluate the company's revenue and earnings growth trends over time. Companies with consistent revenue and earnings growth are better positioned to sustain and increase dividend payments.
- **Profitability Ratios**: Assess profitability ratios, such as gross profit margin, operating margin, and net profit margin, to gauge the company's ability to generate profits from its operations. Higher profit margins indicate greater efficiency and profitability.
- **Debt Levels**: Examine the company's debt levels and debt-to-equity ratio to assess its leverage and financial risk. Companies with high debt levels may face challenges in servicing debt obligations and maintaining dividend payments during economic downturns.
- **Cash Flow**: Analyze the company's cash flow statement to evaluate its ability to generate cash from operating activities. Positive and consistent cash flow is essential for supporting dividend payments and funding growth initiatives.
- **Dividend Coverage Ratio**: Calculate the dividend coverage ratio by dividing the company's earnings per share (EPS) by its dividend per share (DPS). A dividend coverage ratio greater than 1 indicates

that the company's earnings can cover its dividend payments, suggesting financial sustainability.

Interpreting Financial Health Metrics

- **Stable and Growing Metrics**: Look for companies with stable and growing revenue, earnings, and cash flow metrics over time. Consistent growth in these areas indicates a healthy and resilient business model capable of sustaining dividend payments.
- **Low Debt Levels**: Favor companies with low debt levels and conservative leverage ratios. Low debt levels reduce the risk of financial distress and provide greater flexibility for dividend payments and capital allocation.
- **Positive Cash Flow**: Prioritize companies with positive and consistent cash flow from operating activities. Positive cash flow indicates that the company can generate sufficient cash to cover its operating expenses, debt obligations, and dividend payments.

Considerations for Sector and Industry Dynamics

- **Industry Trends**: Consider industry trends and dynamics when evaluating the financial health of a company. Some industries may be more capital-intensive or cyclical, affecting companies' financial metrics and dividend-paying ability.
- **Regulatory Environment**: Assess the regulatory environment and industry-specific risks that may impact companies' financial health and dividend policies. Regulatory changes, technological disruptions, and competitive pressures can affect companies' earnings and cash flow generation.

Assessing the financial health of a company is critical for investors seeking to identify high-quality dividend-paying stocks. By evaluating key financial metrics such as revenue and earnings growth, profitability ratios, debt levels, cash flow, and dividend coverage ratio, investors can gain insights into the company's ability to maintain and grow dividend payments over time. With thorough research and analysis, investors can make informed decisions that align with their investment objectives and risk tolerance, ultimately building a diversified portfolio of dividend stocks poised for long-term success.

3.5 Sector and Industry Considerations

When selecting dividend-paying stocks, it's essential to consider the sector and industry dynamics in which the companies operate. Different sectors and industries have unique characteristics that can impact a company's ability to sustain and grow dividend payments over time. Here's how to navigate sector and industry considerations effectively:

Understanding Sector and Industry Dynamics

- **Cyclical vs. Defensive Sectors**: Different sectors exhibit varying levels of sensitivity to economic cycles. Cyclical sectors, such as technology and consumer discretionary, tend to be more sensitive to economic fluctuations, while defensive sectors, such as utilities and consumer staples, are more resilient during economic downturns.
- **Regulatory Environment**: Consider the regulatory environment and industry-specific regulations that may impact companies within the sector. Regulatory changes can affect companies' costs,

profitability, and dividend policies, making it essential to stay informed about regulatory developments.

- **Competitive Landscape**: Evaluate the competitive landscape within the industry and assess companies' competitive advantages, market position, and pricing power. Companies with strong competitive advantages are better positioned to maintain and grow market share, revenue, and dividends over time.

Sector and Industry Performance

- **Historical Performance**: Analyze the historical performance of sectors and industries to identify trends and patterns. Some sectors may outperform others over certain periods due to macroeconomic factors, industry-specific trends, or investor sentiment.
- **Economic Indicators**: Monitor key economic indicators, such as GDP growth, inflation rates, and unemployment levels, to gauge the health of sectors and industries. Economic conditions can influence consumer spending, business investment, and demand for goods and services, affecting companies' revenue, earnings, and dividend-paying ability.

Sector Rotation Strategies

- **Defensive vs. Growth Sectors**: Consider rotating between defensive and growth sectors based on market conditions and economic outlook. Defensive sectors may outperform during periods of economic uncertainty or market volatility, while growth sectors may offer higher returns during periods of economic expansion.

- **Dividend Yield vs. Dividend Growth**: Determine whether to prioritize dividend yield or dividend growth when selecting dividend-paying stocks. High-yield sectors, such as utilities and real estate investment trusts (REITs), may appeal to income-oriented investors seeking higher dividend yields, while sectors with strong growth prospects, such as technology and healthcare, may offer greater potential for dividend growth.

Sector and industry considerations play a crucial role in the selection of dividend-paying stocks. By understanding the dynamics of different sectors and industries, monitoring economic indicators, and implementing sector rotation strategies, investors can build a diversified portfolio of dividend stocks that align with their investment objectives and risk tolerance. With careful analysis and prudent decision-making, investors can navigate sector and industry dynamics effectively, ultimately maximizing the potential for long-term income and growth from dividend-paying stocks.

Chapter 4: Strategies for Building a Dividend Portfolio

Building a dividend portfolio requires careful planning, research, and execution. In this chapter, we'll explore various strategies that investors can employ to construct a diversified portfolio of dividend-paying stocks tailored to their investment goals and risk tolerance.

1. Dividend Investing Strategies

High Dividend Yield

Investors seeking immediate income often gravitate toward high dividend-yield stocks. These are companies that offer above-average dividend payouts relative to their stock price. While high dividend yield stocks can provide attractive income, investors should exercise caution and ensure that dividend payments are sustainable and backed by strong fundamentals.

Dividend Growth

Dividend growth investing focuses on companies that consistently increase their dividend payments over time. These companies typically have strong financials, stable earnings growth, and a commitment to returning value to shareholders. By investing in dividend growth stocks, investors can benefit from both current income and the potential for future dividend increases.

Dividend Aristocrats

Dividend aristocrats are companies that have a track record of consistently increasing their dividends for at least 25 consecutive years. These companies are often viewed as reliable income generators and are favored by income-oriented investors seeking stability and consistency in dividend payments. Investing in dividend aristocrats can provide a sense of security and confidence in long-term income generation.

2. Sector and Industry Diversification

Diversification is key to building a resilient dividend portfolio that can weather market volatility and economic uncertainties. Investors should spread their investments across different sectors and industries to reduce risk and maximize potential returns. By diversifying across sectors, investors can mitigate the impact of sector-specific risks and capture opportunities for growth and income across various segments of the economy.

3. Reinvesting Dividends

Reinvesting dividends is a powerful strategy for compounding returns and accelerating wealth accumulation over time. Instead of taking dividends in cash, investors can reinvest them to purchase additional shares of dividend-paying stocks. By reinvesting dividends, investors can take advantage of the compounding effect and exponentially grow their investment portfolio over time. Dividend reinvestment plans (DRIPs) offer a convenient and cost-effective way to automate the reinvestment of dividends and maximize the benefits of compounding returns.

4. Dollar-Cost Averaging

Dollar-cost averaging involves investing a fixed amount of money at regular intervals, regardless of market conditions. This strategy helps smooth out the impact of market volatility and reduces the risk of investing a large sum of money at the wrong time. By consistently investing in dividend-paying stocks over time, investors can benefit from fluctuations in stock prices and potentially lower their average cost per share, leading to improved long-term returns.

Building a dividend portfolio requires a thoughtful approach and a deep understanding of various dividend investing strategies. By incorporating high dividend yield, dividend growth, dividend aristocrats, sector diversification, dividend reinvestment, and dollar-cost averaging into their investment approach, investors can construct a well-balanced portfolio that generates consistent income and long-term growth. With careful research, disciplined investing, and a focus on quality dividend-paying stocks, investors can create a path to financial success and achieve their investment goals over time.

4.1 Diversification Strategies

Diversification is a cornerstone of successful investing, especially when building a dividend portfolio. By spreading investments across different sectors, industries, and asset classes, investors can reduce risk and enhance the resilience of their portfolios. Here are several diversification strategies to consider when constructing a dividend portfolio:

1. Sector Diversification

Investors should allocate their investments across various sectors of the economy to reduce exposure to sector-specific risks. Each sector behaves differently in response to economic conditions and market trends, so diversifying across sectors helps balance portfolio performance. Common sectors include:

- **Technology**: Companies involved in technology development and innovation.
- **Healthcare**: Companies in the healthcare industry, including pharmaceuticals, biotechnology, and healthcare services.
- **Consumer Discretionary**: Businesses that provide non-essential goods and services, such as retail, entertainment, and leisure.
- **Utilities**: Companies that provide essential services like electricity, water, and natural gas.
- **Financials**: Banks, insurance companies, and other financial institutions.
- **Consumer Staples**: Companies that produce essential goods like food, beverages, and household products.
- **Industrials**: Manufacturers, transportation companies, and construction firms.
- **Energy**: Companies involved in oil, gas, and renewable energy production.

2. Industry Diversification

Within each sector, investors should further diversify their holdings across different industries to reduce concentration risk. For example, within the technology sector, investors may allocate funds to software, hardware, semiconductor, and internet companies. Similarly, within the healthcare sector, investors can diversify across pharmaceuticals, biotechnology, medical devices, and healthcare services.

3. Geographic Diversification

Geographic diversification involves investing in companies located in different regions and countries around the world. By spreading investments globally, investors can reduce exposure to country-specific risks, political instability, and currency fluctuations. Geographic diversification also provides access to a broader range of investment opportunities and economic growth prospects.

4. Asset Class Diversification

In addition to stocks, investors can diversify their dividend portfolio by allocating funds to other asset classes, such as bonds, real estate investment trusts (REITs), and dividend-paying exchange-traded funds (ETFs). Bonds provide income and stability, while REITs offer exposure to real estate assets. Dividend ETFs provide instant diversification by investing in a basket of dividend-paying stocks across different sectors and industries.

5. Risk-Based Diversification

Investors should also consider their risk tolerance and investment objectives when diversifying their dividend portfolio. Conservative investors may prefer a more defensive approach with a higher allocation to stable, dividend-paying sectors like utilities and consumer staples. Aggressive investors may be willing to take on more risk by investing in growth-oriented sectors like technology and healthcare.

Diversification is essential for building a resilient dividend portfolio that can withstand market volatility and economic uncertainties. By implementing sector, industry, geographic, asset class, and risk-based diversification strategies, investors can reduce risk, enhance portfolio performance, and achieve their long-term investment goals. With careful planning and disciplined execution, diversification can help investors navigate the complexities of the market and build a portfolio that generates consistent income and long-term growth.

4.2 Balancing High Yield vs. Dividend Growth

When constructing a dividend portfolio, investors often face the dilemma of choosing between high-yield stocks that offer immediate income and dividend-growth stocks that provide the potential for higher future dividends. Balancing high yield versus dividend growth requires careful consideration of investment objectives, risk tolerance, and market conditions. Here's how investors can navigate this balancing act effectively:

1. High Yield Stocks

High-yield stocks are companies that offer above-average dividend yields relative to their stock price. These stocks appeal to income-oriented investors seeking immediate cash flow and consistent dividend payments. While high-yield stocks can provide attractive income, they may also carry higher risks, such as dividend cuts or slower dividend growth, particularly if the company's fundamentals deteriorate.

Pros:

- **Immediate Income**: High-yield stocks provide investors with immediate cash flow from dividend payments, which can be useful for covering living expenses or funding retirement.
- **Attractive Yield**: High-yield stocks offer above-average dividend yields, providing a higher percentage return on investment relative to the stock price.

Cons:

- **Risk of Dividend Cuts**: Companies offering high dividend yields may face challenges in sustaining dividend payments over the long term, particularly if their earnings decline or cash flow deteriorates.
- **Limited Growth Potential**: High-yield stocks may have limited potential for capital appreciation, as investors often prioritize income over growth.

2. Dividend Growth Stocks

Dividend growth stocks are companies that consistently increase their dividend payments over time. These stocks appeal to investors seeking a combination of income and capital appreciation. While dividend growth stocks may offer lower initial yields compared to high-yield stocks, they provide the potential for higher future dividends and long-term wealth accumulation through dividend reinvestment and compounding.

Pros:

- **Sustainable Growth**: Dividend growth stocks have a track record of increasing dividends, indicating strong fundamentals and a commitment to returning value to shareholders.
- **Potential for Capital Appreciation**: Dividend growth stocks may experience capital appreciation as a result of improving business performance, earnings growth, and market recognition of their dividend-paying ability.

Cons:

- **Lower Initial Yield**: Dividend growth stocks may offer lower initial yields compared to high-yield stocks, which may be less attractive to income-oriented investors.
- **Volatility**: Dividend growth stocks may exhibit higher volatility compared to high-yield stocks, as investors may be more sensitive to changes in earnings growth and market sentiment.

3. Balancing High Yield and Dividend Growth

To balance high yield versus dividend growth effectively, investors can adopt a diversified approach that incorporates both types of stocks within their portfolio. By diversifying across high-yield and dividend-growth stocks, investors can capture the immediate income from high-yield stocks while benefiting from the potential for future dividend growth and capital appreciation from dividend-growth stocks. Additionally, investors can consider their investment horizon, risk tolerance, and income needs when determining the optimal balance between high yield and dividend growth.

Strategies for Balancing High Yield and Dividend Growth:

- **Core-Satellite Approach**: Allocate a core portion of the portfolio to high-quality dividend growth stocks for long-term wealth accumulation, supplemented by satellite positions in high-yield stocks for immediate income.
- **Dynamic Allocation**: Adjust the allocation between high-yield and dividend-growth stocks based on market conditions, economic outlook, and investment objectives.
- **Dividend Reinvestment**: Reinvest dividends from high-yield stocks into dividend-growth stocks to take advantage of compounding returns and enhance long-term growth potential.

Balancing high yield versus dividend growth is essential for building a resilient dividend portfolio that generates consistent income and long-term growth. By incorporating both high-yield and dividend-growth stocks within their portfolio and adopting a diversified approach, investors can achieve a balanced mix of immediate income and future growth potential. With careful planning and disciplined execution, investors can navigate the complexities of the market and build a portfolio that aligns with their investment goals and risk tolerance.

4.3 Core Dividend Stocks vs. Opportunistic Picks

When building a dividend portfolio, investors often consider incorporating both core dividend stocks and opportunistic picks to achieve a balanced approach that combines stability and growth potential. Core dividend stocks form the foundation of the portfolio, providing consistent income and reliability, while opportunistic picks offer the potential for higher returns through strategic investments. Here's how investors can effectively balance core dividend stocks with opportunistic picks:

1. Core Dividend Stocks

Core dividend stocks are reliable, blue-chip companies with a history of consistent dividend payments and strong fundamentals. These stocks serve as the backbone of the portfolio, providing stability, income, and long-term growth potential. Core dividend stocks typically exhibit the following characteristics:

Characteristics:

- **Stable Dividend History**: Core dividend stocks have a track record of consistently paying dividends, often increasing them over time. They have demonstrated their commitment to returning value to shareholders through various market conditions.
- **Strong Fundamentals**: Core dividend stocks typically have strong financials, including solid revenue, earnings, and cash flow generation. They operate in mature industries with stable demand

and possess competitive advantages that support their market leadership.

- **Resilience in Downturns**: Core dividend stocks tend to be less volatile and more resilient during market downturns compared to growth-oriented or speculative stocks. They provide investors with a sense of security and confidence in their ability to weather economic uncertainties.

2. Opportunistic Picks

Opportunistic picks are stocks that offer higher growth potential or special situations that may lead to outsized returns. These stocks may not have a long track record of dividend payments but present unique opportunities for capital appreciation or income generation. Opportunistic picks typically exhibit the following characteristics:

Characteristics:

- **Potential for Growth**: Opportunistic picks may operate in emerging industries, have innovative business models, or possess disruptive technologies that offer significant growth potential. These stocks may appeal to investors seeking higher returns and willing to tolerate higher risk.
- **Special Situations**: Opportunistic picks may include turnaround stories, undervalued companies, or companies undergoing restructuring or strategic initiatives. These special situations can create opportunities for investors to capitalize on short-term catalysts or market inefficiencies.

- **Higher Volatility**: Opportunistic picks tend to be more volatile and speculative compared to core dividend stocks. They may experience greater price fluctuations in response to market events, earnings reports, or company-specific news.

3. Balancing Core Dividend Stocks and Opportunistic Picks

To balance core dividend stocks with opportunistic picks effectively, investors should consider their investment objectives, risk tolerance, and time horizon. A diversified approach that combines both types of stocks can help investors achieve a balanced portfolio that provides income, stability, and growth potential. Here are some strategies for balancing core dividend stocks and opportunistic picks:

Strategies:

- **Core-Satellite Approach**: Allocate a core portion of the portfolio to stable, blue-chip dividend stocks for income and stability, supplemented by satellite positions in opportunistic picks for growth potential.
- **Dynamic Allocation**: Adjust the allocation between core dividend stocks and opportunistic picks based on market conditions, economic outlook, and investment opportunities. Increase exposure to opportunistic picks during periods of market optimism and reduce exposure during periods of uncertainty or volatility.
- **Risk Management**: Implement risk management strategies, such as position sizing, diversification, and stop-loss orders, to mitigate the risks associated with opportunistic picks. Set clear investment

criteria and exit strategies for opportunistic picks to protect capital and minimize losses.

Balancing core dividend stocks with opportunistic picks is essential for building a diversified dividend portfolio that combines stability and growth potential. By incorporating both types of stocks within their portfolio and adopting a disciplined approach to asset allocation and risk management, investors can achieve their investment goals while managing risk effectively. With careful planning, research, and execution, investors can navigate the complexities of the market and build a portfolio that provides income, stability, and long-term growth.

4.4 International Dividend Stocks

International dividend stocks offer investors the opportunity to diversify their dividend portfolio beyond domestic markets and gain exposure to global growth opportunities. Investing in international dividend stocks can provide additional income, diversification benefits, and access to economies and industries not available domestically. Here's what investors need to know about international dividend stocks:

Benefits of International Dividend Stocks

1. **Diversification**: International dividend stocks provide diversification benefits by reducing exposure to domestic market risks and currency fluctuations. Investing in companies from different countries and regions can help mitigate the impact of local economic and geopolitical events on the portfolio.

2. **Growth Opportunities**: International dividend stocks offer exposure to economies with different growth rates, stages of development, and industry compositions. Emerging markets, in particular, may present higher growth potential compared to mature markets, providing opportunities for capital appreciation and dividend growth.
3. **Currency Hedge**: Investing in international dividend stocks can serve as a currency hedge against fluctuations in the domestic currency. Holding assets denominated in foreign currencies can help protect the portfolio's purchasing power and provide a hedge against inflation and currency devaluation.

Considerations for Investing in International Dividend Stocks

1. **Currency Risk**: Investing in international dividend stocks exposes investors to currency risk, as fluctuations in exchange rates can impact the value of investments denominated in foreign currencies. Investors should consider currency hedging strategies or focus on countries with stable currencies to mitigate currency risk.
2. **Political and Regulatory Risks**: International dividend stocks are subject to political and regulatory risks specific to the countries in which they operate. Factors such as changes in government policies, regulatory environments, and geopolitical tensions can affect the performance of international stocks.
3. **Tax Implications**: Investors should be aware of the tax implications of investing in international dividend stocks, including withholding taxes on dividends and capital gains taxes in foreign jurisdictions. Tax treaties between countries may mitigate double taxation, but investors should consult with tax professionals to understand their tax obligations.

Strategies for Investing in International Dividend Stocks

1. **Research and Due Diligence**: Conduct thorough research and due diligence on international companies, including their business models, financials, dividend history, and corporate governance practices. Consider factors such as competitive positioning, industry trends, and economic fundamentals when evaluating international dividend stocks.
2. **Diversification**: Diversify across countries, regions, and industries to spread risk and capture opportunities for growth and income. Avoid overconcentration in any single country or region to reduce exposure to country-specific risks.
3. **Consider Exchange-Traded Funds (ETFs)**: Consider investing in international dividend-focused ETFs, which offer diversified exposure to a basket of international dividend stocks. ETFs provide convenient and cost-effective access to international markets and can help mitigate individual stock risk.

International dividend stocks can play a valuable role in a diversified dividend portfolio, offering additional income, growth opportunities, and diversification benefits. By carefully considering the benefits, risks, and strategies for investing in international dividend stocks, investors can enhance their portfolio's resilience and potential for long-term returns. With proper research, due diligence, and risk management, investors can harness the benefits of international diversification and build a portfolio that generates consistent income and growth across global markets.

4.5 Tax Considerations

Tax considerations play a crucial role in dividend investing, as they can impact the after-tax returns and overall performance of a dividend portfolio. Understanding the tax implications of dividend income, capital gains, and investment vehicles is essential for maximizing tax efficiency and optimizing investment outcomes. Here are several key tax considerations for dividend investors:

1. Dividend Taxation

- **Qualified vs. Ordinary Dividends**: Dividends can be classified as either qualified or ordinary, depending on the holding period of the underlying stock. Qualified dividends are subject to lower tax rates, similar to long-term capital gains rates, while ordinary dividends are taxed at the investor's ordinary income tax rates.
- **Tax Rates**: As of the latest tax laws, qualified dividends are taxed at preferential tax rates ranging from 0% to 20%, depending on the investor's tax bracket. Ordinary dividends are taxed at the investor's ordinary income tax rates, which can be significantly higher.
- **Holding Period**: To qualify for preferential tax rates on dividends, investors must meet certain holding period requirements, typically holding the underlying stock for more than 60 days during the 121 days surrounding the ex-dividend date.

2. Capital Gains Taxation

- **Long-Term vs. Short-Term Capital Gains**: Capital gains from the sale of stocks held for more than one year are classified as long-term capital gains and taxed at preferential rates. Capital gains from stocks held for one year or less are classified as short-term capital gains and taxed at the investor's ordinary income tax rates.
- **Tax Rates**: Long-term capital gains are taxed at preferential rates ranging from 0% to 20%, depending on the investor's tax bracket. Short-term capital gains are taxed at the investor's ordinary income tax rates, which can be significantly higher.
- **Tax-Loss Harvesting**: Investors can offset capital gains taxes by selling investments at a loss to realize capital losses. These losses can be used to offset capital gains, reducing the investor's overall tax liability.

3. Tax-Efficient Investment Vehicles

- **Qualified Retirement Accounts**: Investing in dividend-paying stocks within qualified retirement accounts, such as 401(k)s and IRAs, can provide tax-deferred or tax-free growth, depending on the account type. Dividend income and capital gains generated within these accounts are not subject to immediate taxation, allowing for greater compounding potential.
- **Tax-Advantaged Accounts**: Consider investing in tax-advantaged accounts, such as Roth IRAs and Health Savings Accounts (HSAs), which offer tax-free withdrawals on qualified distributions. Dividend income and capital gains generated within

these accounts can grow tax-free, providing significant tax benefits in retirement.

4. Minimizing Tax Liability

- **Asset Location**: Place tax-efficient investments, such as dividend-paying stocks and tax-exempt bonds, in taxable accounts, while holding tax-inefficient investments, such as high-turnover mutual funds, in tax-advantaged accounts. This strategy can help minimize tax liability and maximize after-tax returns.
- **Tax-Loss Harvesting**: Take advantage of tax-loss harvesting opportunities to offset capital gains taxes and reduce overall tax liability. Selling investments at a loss can help capture tax deductions and improve after-tax returns.

Tax considerations are an integral part of dividend investing and can significantly impact investment outcomes. By understanding the tax implications of dividend income, capital gains, and investment vehicles, investors can implement tax-efficient strategies to maximize after-tax returns and optimize the performance of their dividend portfolios. With careful planning, research, and execution, investors can navigate the complexities of the tax code and build a dividend portfolio that generates consistent income and long-term growth while minimizing tax liability.

Chapter 5: Managing and Monitoring Your Dividend Portfolio

In the journey of building and nurturing your dividend portfolio, the process doesn't end with just picking the right stocks. Managing and monitoring your investments are equally crucial aspects that demand your attention and care. In this chapter, we delve into the intricacies of effectively managing and monitoring your dividend portfolio to ensure its growth and sustainability.

The Importance of Active Management

One common misconception among investors, particularly beginners, is that once they've assembled their portfolio, they can sit back and watch their money grow passively. While the concept of passive income through dividends is appealing, successful investors understand the need for active management.

Active management involves regularly assessing your portfolio's performance, making adjustments as necessary, and staying informed about market trends and economic indicators. It's about being proactive rather than reactive, ensuring that your investments align with your financial goals and risk tolerance.

Establishing Clear Objectives

Before delving into the intricacies of managing your dividend portfolio, it's essential to establish clear objectives. Ask yourself: What are your financial goals? Are you investing for retirement, wealth accumulation, or generating supplemental income? Understanding your objectives will guide your investment decisions and help you stay focused amidst market fluctuations.

Diversification and Rebalancing

Diversification is a cornerstone of successful investing, and it applies equally to dividend portfolios. By spreading your investments across various sectors, industries, and asset classes, you mitigate risk and enhance the potential for long-term growth. Regularly rebalancing your portfolio ensures that your asset allocation remains aligned with your risk tolerance and investment objectives.

Monitoring Dividend Performance

Monitoring the performance of dividend-paying stocks is integral to managing your portfolio effectively. Keep track of dividend yields, payout ratios, dividend growth rates, and dividend coverage ratios. Evaluate whether companies are consistently generating sufficient earnings to sustain and grow their dividends over time.

Staying Informed

In today's fast-paced financial markets, staying informed is paramount. Subscribe to financial news outlets, follow reputable analysts and investment gurus, and utilize financial tools and resources to stay abreast of market developments. Remember, knowledge is power, and informed decisions lead to better investment outcomes.

Harnessing Technology

Technology has revolutionized the way we manage and monitor our investments. Utilize investment apps, portfolio trackers, and online brokerage platforms to streamline your investment process. Take advantage of features like automatic dividend reinvestment plans (DRIPs) and dividend tracking tools to maximize the efficiency of your portfolio management.

The Emotional Aspect

Finally, managing a dividend portfolio isn't just about numbers; it also involves managing emotions. Market volatility can evoke fear, greed, and anxiety, leading to impulsive decisions that may harm your portfolio's performance. Stay disciplined, stick to your investment strategy, and avoid making rash decisions based on short-term market fluctuations.

By establishing clear objectives, diversifying your investments, staying informed, and harnessing technology, you can navigate the complexities of the financial markets and build a resilient portfolio that stands the test of time. Remember, successful investing is a journey, not a destination, and continuous monitoring and adjustment are key to achieving your financial goals.

5.1 Regular Portfolio Review

Regularly reviewing your portfolio is a fundamental aspect of effective portfolio management. Just as you would service a car to ensure it runs smoothly, conducting periodic portfolio reviews helps ensure your investments are on track to meet your financial objectives. In this section, we'll explore the importance of regular portfolio reviews and provide a framework for conducting them effectively.

Why Regular Portfolio Reviews Matter

The financial markets are dynamic and ever-changing, influenced by a myriad of factors such as economic conditions, geopolitical events, and industry trends. As such, what may have been a sound investment decision yesterday may not hold today. Regular portfolio reviews enable you to adapt to evolving market conditions, identify underperforming assets, and capitalize on new opportunities.

Frequency of Reviews

The frequency of portfolio reviews can vary depending on individual circumstances and investment goals. However, as a general rule of thumb, conducting a comprehensive review at least once a quarter is recommended. This allows you to stay informed about your portfolio's performance and make timely adjustments as necessary. Additionally, conducting an annual review at the end of each fiscal year can provide valuable insights into your long-term investment strategy.

Key Components of a Portfolio Review

A thorough portfolio review encompasses several key components, including:

- **Performance Evaluation**: Assess the overall performance of your portfolio relative to your investment objectives and benchmarks. Analyze both absolute returns and risk-adjusted returns to gain a comprehensive understanding of how your investments are performing.
- **Asset Allocation**: Review your portfolio's asset allocation to ensure it remains aligned with your risk tolerance and investment objectives. Rebalance your portfolio if necessary to maintain optimal asset allocation ratios.
- **Individual Security Analysis**: Evaluate the performance of individual securities within your portfolio. Identify underperforming assets and assess whether there are any fundamental or technical factors impacting their performance.
- **Dividend Analysis**: If your portfolio consists of dividend-paying stocks, analyze the performance of dividend distributions. Assess whether dividend income is meeting expectations and evaluate the sustainability of dividend payments.
- **Risk Management**: Review your portfolio's risk exposure and assess whether it aligns with your risk tolerance. Identify any concentration risks or correlations among assets that may pose a threat to portfolio stability.

Conducting the Review

When conducting a portfolio review, it's essential to approach it with a systematic and disciplined mindset. Start by gathering relevant financial data, including portfolio statements, performance reports, and dividend records. Utilize analytical tools and software to streamline the review process and identify trends or anomalies in your portfolio's performance.

Once you've collected the necessary data, take a step back and assess your portfolio's overall health. Ask yourself whether your current investment strategy is still appropriate given prevailing market conditions and your financial objectives. Be prepared to make adjustments to your portfolio if necessary, whether it involves reallocating assets, trimming underperforming positions, or exploring new investment opportunities.

In conclusion, regular portfolio reviews are essential for maintaining the health and vitality of your investment portfolio. By conducting thorough reviews at regular intervals, you can ensure your investments remain aligned with your financial goals, minimize risks, and capitalize on growth opportunities. Remember, investing is an ongoing process, and staying actively engaged with your portfolio is key to achieving long-term success.

5.2 Analyzing Quarterly Earnings Reports

Analyzing quarterly earnings reports is a crucial aspect of managing a dividend portfolio effectively. These reports provide valuable insights into the financial health and performance of the companies in which you've invested. In this section, we'll explore why quarterly earnings reports are important and outline a framework for analyzing them.

Importance of Quarterly Earnings Reports

Quarterly earnings reports offer investors a snapshot of a company's performance over a specific period, typically three months. They provide key financial metrics such as revenue, earnings per share (EPS), net income, and operating margins, allowing investors to evaluate a company's profitability, growth trajectory, and operational efficiency.

For dividend investors, quarterly earnings reports are particularly significant as they provide insights into the company's ability to sustain and grow dividend payments over time. By analyzing earnings reports, investors can assess whether a company's earnings are sufficient to support dividend distributions and identify any potential red flags that may impact dividend sustainability.

Key Components of Quarterly Earnings Reports

When analyzing quarterly earnings reports, focus on the following key components:

- **Revenue Growth**: Evaluate the company's top-line growth by examining its revenue figures. Look for consistent revenue growth quarter-over-quarter or year-over-year, as it indicates strong demand for the company's products or services.
- **Earnings Per Share (EPS)**: Assess the company's profitability by analyzing its EPS, which represents the portion of the company's profit allocated to each outstanding share of common stock. Compare current EPS figures to analyst estimates and previous

quarters' performance to gauge whether the company is meeting expectations.

- **Net Income**: Examine the company's net income, which reflects its total earnings after deducting expenses such as operating costs, taxes, and interest payments. A positive net income indicates profitability, while a negative net income may signal financial distress.
- **Dividend Payout Ratio**: Calculate the company's dividend payout ratio, which measures the percentage of earnings paid out as dividends to shareholders. A lower payout ratio indicates that the company retains more earnings for reinvestment or future dividends, while a higher payout ratio may suggest that the company is distributing a significant portion of its earnings as dividends.
- **Operating Margins**: Evaluate the company's operating margins, which measure its profitability relative to revenue. Higher operating margins indicate greater efficiency in generating profits from sales.

Conducting the Analysis

When analyzing quarterly earnings reports, start by reviewing the company's earnings release and accompanying financial statements, including the income statement, balance sheet, and cash flow statement. Pay attention to management commentary and guidance regarding future performance and strategic initiatives.

Utilize financial analysis tools and ratios to assess the company's financial health and performance relative to its industry peers and benchmarks. Look for trends or anomalies in key financial metrics and seek explanations for any deviations from expectations.

Finally, consider the broader economic and market context in which the company operates. Factor in macroeconomic trends, industry dynamics, and competitive pressures that may impact the company's performance and prospects.

In conclusion, analyzing quarterly earnings reports is an essential skill for dividend investors seeking to make informed investment decisions. By carefully evaluating key financial metrics and understanding the broader market context, investors can assess the financial health and performance of the companies in their dividend portfolios. Remember, thorough analysis and attention to detail are key to identifying high-quality dividend stocks with the potential for long-term growth and income.

5.3 Adjusting for Dividend Cuts or Suspensions

Dividend cuts or suspensions can be unsettling for investors, especially those relying on dividend income to meet their financial goals. However, effectively managing your dividend portfolio requires the ability to adapt to changing circumstances and make necessary adjustments when faced with dividend cuts or suspensions. In this section, we'll explore strategies for navigating dividend cuts or suspensions and minimizing their impact on your portfolio.

Understanding the Reasons behind Dividend Cuts or Suspensions

Before taking any action, it's essential to understand the reasons behind dividend cuts or suspensions. Companies may reduce or suspend dividends for various reasons, including:

- **Financial Distress**: Companies experiencing financial difficulties may cut or suspend dividends to preserve cash and strengthen their balance sheets.
- **Cyclical or Sector-Specific Factors**: Economic downturns or industry-specific challenges may prompt companies to trim dividends temporarily until conditions improve.
- **Strategic Priorities**: Companies may prioritize reinvesting cash into growth initiatives or debt reduction over paying dividends to shareholders.

By understanding the underlying reasons for dividend cuts or suspensions, investors can better assess the potential impact on their portfolios and make informed decisions accordingly.

Evaluating the Impact on Your Portfolio

When faced with dividend cuts or suspensions, evaluate the impact on your portfolio's overall income and total return. Consider the following factors:

- **Income Reduction**: Calculate the percentage reduction in dividend income resulting from the cut or suspension. Assess whether the remaining dividends from other holdings are sufficient to offset the loss in income.
- **Total Return Impact**: Evaluate the impact on your portfolio's total return, taking into account changes in stock prices following the dividend announcement. Determine whether the reduction in dividend income is offset by capital appreciation or if it significantly affects your portfolio's overall return.

Adjusting Your Portfolio Strategy

Based on your assessment, consider adjusting your portfolio strategy to mitigate the impact of dividend cuts or suspensions. Possible strategies include:

- **Diversification**: Ensure your portfolio is well-diversified across different sectors and industries to reduce the impact of dividend cuts or suspensions from any single holding.
- **Quality Over Yield**: Prioritize investing in high-quality dividend-paying companies with strong fundamentals and a track record of consistent dividend payments. Focus on companies with sustainable business models, robust cash flows, and prudent dividend policies.
- **Reinvestment**: Consider reinvesting dividends from other holdings into companies with stable or growing dividends to offset the loss in income from dividend cuts or suspensions.
- **Monitoring and Adjustment**: Continuously monitor your portfolio for changes in dividend policies or financial health indicators that may signal potential dividend cuts or suspensions. Be prepared to adjust your holdings accordingly to mitigate risk and capitalize on new opportunities.

Maintaining a Long-Term Perspective

Finally, maintain a long-term perspective when managing your dividend portfolio. While dividend cuts or suspensions may be disappointing in the short term, focus on the underlying fundamentals of your investments and their potential for long-term growth and income generation. By staying disciplined and adaptable, you can navigate through challenging periods and position your portfolio for success over the long term.

In conclusion, adjusting for dividend cuts or suspensions is an essential aspect of managing a dividend portfolio effectively. By understanding the reasons behind dividend cuts or suspensions, evaluating their impact on your portfolio, and implementing appropriate adjustments to your investment strategy, you can minimize their adverse effects and position your portfolio for long-term success. Remember, maintaining a diversified portfolio of high-quality dividend-paying stocks and staying focused on your long-term financial goals are key principles of successful dividend investing.

5.4 Reinvesting Dividends vs. Taking Cash

One of the decisions dividend investors often face is whether to reinvest dividends back into the underlying stocks or to take them as cash. Both options have their merits, and the choice depends on individual financial goals, investment strategy, and current market conditions. In this section, we'll explore the considerations involved in reinvesting dividends versus taking cash and provide insights to help you make an informed decision.

1. Reinvesting Dividends

Compounding Growth:

Reinvesting dividends allows you to harness the power of compounding growth. By reinvesting dividends into additional shares of the same stock or other dividend-paying investments, you can potentially accelerate the growth of your portfolio over time. Compounding enables your investment to generate earnings not only on the original principal but also on the reinvested dividends, leading to exponential growth over the long term.

Dollar-Cost Averaging:

Reinvesting dividends through a dividend reinvestment plan (DRIP) enables you to practice dollar-cost averaging. With dollar-cost averaging, you invest a fixed dollar amount regularly, regardless of market fluctuations. By automatically reinvesting dividends, you buy more shares when prices are low and fewer shares when prices are high, resulting in a lower average cost per share over time.

Long-Term Wealth Accumulation:

For investors focused on long-term wealth accumulation, reinvesting dividends can be an effective strategy. By reinvesting dividends and allowing your investments to grow over time, you can potentially build a larger portfolio and generate significant wealth through capital appreciation and compound interest.

2. Taking Cash

Supplemental Income:

For investors seeking regular income to meet living expenses or other financial obligations, taking dividends as cash provides a steady stream of income. Dividend payments can serve as a reliable source of passive income, supplementing other sources of revenue such as salary or retirement benefits.

Flexibility and Liquidity:

Taking dividends as cash offers flexibility and liquidity, allowing you to use the funds as needed for expenses, investment opportunities, or other financial goals. Cash dividends provide immediate access to funds without having to sell shares, making them suitable for investors who value liquidity and prefer to maintain control over their cash flow.

Portfolio Diversification:

Taking dividends as cash provides the flexibility to reinvest the funds in other investment opportunities outside of the dividend-paying stocks in your portfolio. This allows you to diversify your investments across different asset classes, sectors, or industries, reducing concentration risk and potentially enhancing portfolio returns.

Considerations for Decision-Making

When deciding whether to reinvest dividends or take them as cash, consider the following factors:

- **Financial Goals**: Evaluate your financial goals and investment objectives. Determine whether you prioritize long-term wealth accumulation and capital appreciation or require immediate income to meet current expenses.
- **Risk Tolerance**: Assess your risk tolerance and investment horizon. Reinvesting dividends may be suitable for investors with a long-term investment horizon and a higher risk tolerance, while taking cash dividends may be preferable for those seeking income stability and capital preservation.
- **Tax Implications**: Consider the tax implications of reinvesting dividends versus taking them as cash. Reinvested dividends may be subject to taxation if they result in the acquisition of additional shares, whereas cash dividends are typically taxable in the year they are received.
- **Market Conditions**: Evaluate current market conditions and economic outlook. In bullish markets, reinvesting dividends may capitalize on growth opportunities, while in volatile or bearish markets, taking cash dividends may provide stability and liquidity.

In conclusion, the decision to reinvest dividends or take them as cash depends on individual circumstances, financial goals, and market conditions. Reinvesting dividends offers the potential for compounding growth and long-term wealth accumulation while taking cash dividends provides supplemental income, flexibility, and liquidity. By carefully considering your investment objectives, risk tolerance, and tax implications, you can determine the most suitable approach for managing your dividend portfolio and achieving your financial goals. Remember, there is no one-size-fits-all solution, and the optimal strategy may evolve as your circumstances and objectives change.

5.5 Using Technology and Tools

Technology has revolutionized the way investors manage their dividend portfolios, providing access to a wealth of information, analytical tools, and investment platforms. In this section, we'll explore the various ways technology and tools can enhance the management of your dividend portfolio and empower you to make informed investment decisions.

Portfolio Management Software

Portfolio management software offers a comprehensive solution for tracking and analyzing your dividend investments. These platforms allow you to consolidate all your investment accounts, track portfolio performance, monitor dividend income, and generate detailed reports. With features such as portfolio rebalancing, performance benchmarking, and tax optimization, portfolio management software simplifies the investment process and provides valuable insights into your portfolio's health and performance.

Investment Apps

Investment apps have made investing more accessible and convenient than ever before. With intuitive interfaces and mobile-friendly designs, investment apps enable you to monitor your dividend portfolio on the go, execute trades, and access real-time market data and news. Many investment apps also offer educational resources, investment research, and customizable alerts to keep you informed and empowered to make sound investment decisions.

Dividend Tracking Tools

Dividend tracking tools allow you to monitor dividend payments from your portfolio holdings and analyze dividend income over time. These tools provide detailed dividend histories, payout schedules, and dividend yield calculations for individual stocks and entire portfolios. By tracking dividend payments and reinvestment opportunities, dividend tracking tools help you optimize your portfolio for income generation and long-term growth.

Automatic Dividend Reinvestment Plans (DRIPs)

Automatic Dividend Reinvestment Plans (DRIPs) enable you to reinvest dividends automatically into additional shares of the same stock or mutual fund without incurring trading fees. DRIPs harness the power of compounding growth, allowing you to reinvest dividends consistently over time and accumulate more shares at potentially lower costs. By enrolling in DRIPs, you can maximize the efficiency of your dividend reinvestment strategy and accelerate the growth of your portfolio.

Robo-Advisors

Robo-advisors leverage technology and algorithms to provide automated investment management services at a fraction of the cost of traditional financial advisors. These platforms assess your risk tolerance, investment goals, and time horizon to create a diversified portfolio of ETFs or index funds tailored to your individual needs. Robo-advisors offer features such as automatic rebalancing, tax-loss harvesting, and goal-based investing, making them an attractive option for investors seeking low-cost, hands-off portfolio management.

In conclusion, technology and tools play a pivotal role in enhancing the management of your dividend portfolio and empowering you to achieve your investment goals. From portfolio management software and investment apps to dividend tracking tools and automatic DRIPs, there is a plethora of resources available to help you monitor, analyze, and optimize your dividend investments. By leveraging technology effectively, you can streamline your investment process, make informed decisions, and maximize the potential for long-term wealth accumulation and income generation.

Chapter 6: Advanced Dividend Investing Techniques

Welcome to the realm of advanced dividend investing techniques. In this chapter, we'll explore sophisticated strategies and tactics designed to elevate your dividend investing game to the next level. Whether you're a seasoned investor looking to enhance your portfolio's performance or a novice eager to learn advanced techniques, this chapter will provide valuable insights and actionable guidance to help you achieve your investment objectives.

1. Dividend Growth Investing

Dividend growth investing focuses on investing in companies with a track record of consistently increasing their dividend payments over time. By selecting companies with strong fundamentals, sustainable earnings growth, and a commitment to returning capital to shareholders, dividend growth investors aim to capitalize on the power of compounding dividends. This strategy emphasizes quality over yield, prioritizing companies with the potential for long-term dividend growth and capital appreciation.

2. Dividend Reinvestment Strategies

Dividend reinvestment strategies aim to maximize the efficiency of dividend reinvestment and accelerate the growth of your portfolio. Techniques such as automatic dividend reinvestment plans (DRIPs), partial dividend reinvestment, and strategic reinvestment timing allow investors to capitalize on compounding growth and optimize their dividend reinvestment strategy. By reinvesting dividends systematically and strategically, investors can harness the power of compounding to build wealth over time.

3. Dividend Capture Strategies

Dividend capture strategies involve capitalizing on short-term fluctuations in stock prices around ex-dividend dates to capture dividend income. Techniques such as dividend stripping, dividend arbitrage, and dividend capture trades enable investors to generate income by buying dividend-paying stocks before the ex-dividend date and selling them shortly thereafter. While dividend capture strategies can be profitable, they require careful timing, risk management, and an understanding of market dynamics.

4. Sector Rotation

Sector rotation involves adjusting your portfolio allocation based on prevailing economic conditions and sector performance trends. By rotating into sectors poised for growth and out of sectors facing headwinds, investors can optimize their portfolio's risk-return profile and capitalize on sector-specific opportunities. Dividend investors may use sector rotation strategies to overweight sectors with high dividend yields or defensive characteristics during economic downturns and rotate into growth-oriented sectors during expansionary periods.

5. Option Strategies for Dividend Enhancement

Option strategies offer advanced techniques for enhancing dividend income and managing portfolio risk. Strategies such as covered calls, cash-secured puts, and dividend collar trades allow investors to generate additional income from their dividend-paying stocks while providing downside protection and enhancing overall portfolio yield. While option strategies can be complex and carry additional risks, they offer opportunities for income generation and risk mitigation in a diversified dividend portfolio.

In conclusion, advanced dividend investing techniques offer sophisticated strategies and tactics for enhancing portfolio income, capital appreciation, and risk management. Whether you're interested in dividend growth investing, dividend reinvestment strategies, dividend capture techniques, sector rotation, or option strategies, there are ample opportunities to optimize your dividend portfolio and achieve your investment goals. By leveraging advanced techniques and staying disciplined in your approach, you can unlock the full potential of dividend investing and build a resilient portfolio capable of generating sustainable income and long-term wealth.

6.1 Dividend Aristocrats and Kings

Dividend Aristocrats and Dividend Kings are esteemed groups of companies that have demonstrated exceptional commitment to dividend growth over time. In this section, we'll delve into what sets these elite dividend-paying stocks apart and explore the strategies for incorporating them into your investment portfolio.

Dividend Aristocrats

Dividend Aristocrats are S&P 500 index constituents that have increased their dividend payouts for at least 25 consecutive years. These companies have weathered economic downturns, market fluctuations, and industry challenges while consistently rewarding shareholders with rising dividends. Dividend Aristocrats typically represent established blue-chip companies with strong fundamentals, stable cash flows, and a history of prudent capital allocation. Investing in Dividend Aristocrats offers investors the opportunity to gain exposure to companies with proven track records of dividend growth and stability.

Dividend Kings

Dividend Kings represent an even more exclusive group of companies that have raised their dividends for at least 50 consecutive years. These companies are revered for their unparalleled commitment to returning capital to shareholders and their ability to navigate through decades of economic cycles and market volatility. Dividend Kings are often household names with enduring brands, wide economic moats, and resilient business models. Investing in Dividend Kings provides investors with a sense of confidence and security, knowing they're aligned with companies that have stood the test of time and consistently delivered value to shareholders.

Strategies for Incorporating Dividend Aristocrats and Kings

- **Income Generation**: Dividend Aristocrats and Kings are prized for their ability to generate steady and growing income for investors. Incorporating these companies into your portfolio can provide a reliable stream of dividend income, making them suitable for income-oriented investors seeking passive income streams to support their financial goals.
- **Capital Appreciation**: In addition to income generation, Dividend Aristocrats and Kings have historically delivered competitive total returns through capital appreciation. These companies often outperform the broader market over the long term, driven by their consistent dividend growth, earnings stability, and shareholder-friendly policies.
- **Portfolio Stability**: Dividend Aristocrats and Kings tend to exhibit lower volatility and downside risk compared to non-dividend-paying stocks or companies with inconsistent dividend histories. Including these companies in your portfolio can enhance overall stability and resilience, particularly during periods of market uncertainty or economic downturns.
- **Long-Term Growth**: Investing in Dividend Aristocrats and Kings aligns with a long-term growth strategy, as these companies have demonstrated the ability to compound dividends and shareholder wealth over extended periods. By reinvesting dividends and allowing investments to grow over time, investors can capitalize on the power of compounding and achieve long-term financial success.

In conclusion, Dividend Aristocrats and Kings represent the pinnacle of dividend investing, embodying qualities of stability, reliability, and wealth creation. Incorporating these esteemed companies into your investment portfolio can provide a solid foundation for income generation, capital appreciation, and long-term growth. Whether you're seeking reliable dividend income, portfolio stability, or exposure to companies with proven track records of success, Dividend Aristocrats and Kings offer compelling opportunities for investors looking to achieve their investment objectives.

6.2 High-Yield Dividend Stocks: Risks and Rewards

High-yield dividend stocks are often enticing for investors seeking robust income streams, but they come with their own set of risks and rewards. In this section, we'll explore the dynamics of high-yield dividend stocks, the potential benefits they offer, and the associated risks investors should consider.

Rewards of High-Yield Dividend Stocks

- **Income Generation**: High-yield dividend stocks provide investors with above-average dividend yields, offering the potential for significant income generation. These stocks are particularly appealing to income-oriented investors who rely on dividends to meet living expenses or supplement other sources of income.
- **Total Return Potential**: In addition to income generation, high-yield dividend stocks can contribute to total return through dividend reinvestment and capital appreciation. Reinvesting dividends can compound returns over time, while capital appreciation can enhance overall portfolio performance and wealth accumulation.

- **Diversification**: High-yield dividend stocks often span a wide range of sectors and industries, providing investors with opportunities for portfolio diversification. By investing in a diversified portfolio of high-yield dividend stocks, investors can spread risk and mitigate exposure to sector-specific or company-specific factors.

Risks of High-Yield Dividend Stocks

- **Dividend Sustainability**: High-yield dividend stocks may carry elevated risks of dividend cuts or suspensions, particularly if dividend payouts exceed earnings or cash flow generation. Investors should assess the sustainability of high dividend yields by evaluating factors such as payout ratios, earnings growth prospects, and cash flow stability.
- **Market Volatility**: High-yield dividend stocks may exhibit higher volatility compared to low-yield or non-dividend-paying stocks, particularly during periods of market uncertainty or economic downturns. Investors should be prepared for fluctuations in stock prices and potential declines in portfolio value, especially if market conditions deteriorate.
- **Company-Specific Risks**: High-yield dividend stocks may be exposed to company-specific risks such as industry competition, regulatory challenges, or management issues. Investors should conduct thorough due diligence on individual companies to assess their financial health, competitive positioning, and dividend sustainability before investing.

Strategies for Investing in High-Yield Dividend Stocks

- **Focus on Quality**: Prioritize high-yield dividend stocks with strong fundamentals, sustainable business models, and proven track records of dividend payments. Look for companies with healthy balance sheets, consistent earnings growth, and prudent dividend policies to minimize the risk of dividend cuts or suspensions.

- **Diversify Portfolio**: Diversify your portfolio across different sectors, industries, and geographic regions to spread risk and mitigate exposure to company-specific or sector-specific factors. Avoid overconcentration in high-yield dividend stocks or sectors with elevated risks of dividend cuts or economic sensitivity.

- **Monitor Dividend Health**: Continuously monitor the financial health and dividend sustainability of high-yield dividend stocks in your portfolio. Stay informed about changes in company fundamentals, earnings outlook, and dividend policies, and be prepared to adjust your holdings accordingly to protect your income stream and portfolio value.

In conclusion, high-yield dividend stocks offer the potential for robust income generation and total return, but they also come with elevated risks that investors should carefully consider. By understanding the dynamics of high-yield dividend stocks, assessing dividend sustainability, and implementing prudent investment strategies, investors can capitalize on the rewards while mitigating the risks associated with these investments. Whether you're seeking income, total return, or portfolio diversification, high-yield dividend stocks can play a valuable role in achieving your investment objectives when approached with diligence and caution.

6.3 Options Strategies for Dividend Investors

Options strategies offer dividend investors a versatile toolkit for enhancing income, managing risk, and optimizing portfolio performance. In this section, we'll explore various options strategies tailored specifically for dividend investors, along with their benefits and considerations.

Covered Calls

Covered calls involve selling call options against existing stock holdings in your portfolio. By selling call options, investors can generate additional income in the form of premiums while potentially limiting upside potential. Covered calls are often employed by dividend investors to enhance income from their stock holdings, particularly in sideways or slightly bullish market conditions. However, investors should be aware that selling covered calls caps potential gains if the stock price rises above the strike price of the call option.

Cash-Secured Puts

Cash-secured puts involve selling put options against cash reserves set aside to purchase the underlying stock if assigned. By selling put options, investors can generate income in the form of premiums while potentially acquiring shares at a lower price if the stock price declines. Cash-secured puts are often used by dividend investors to enter or add to positions in dividend-paying stocks at attractive prices. However, investors should be prepared to purchase the underlying stock if assigned, potentially tying up capital and increasing exposure to market fluctuations.

Dividend Collar Trades

Dividend collar trades involve simultaneously selling covered calls and buying protective puts to hedge against downside risk. By implementing a dividend collar, investors can generate income from covered calls while protecting their stock holdings from potential losses. Dividend collar trades are particularly suitable for dividend investors seeking to enhance income while maintaining downside protection in volatile or uncertain market conditions. However, the cost of purchasing protective puts may reduce the overall income potential from the strategy.

Benefits of Options Strategies for Dividend Investors

- **Income Generation**: Options strategies offer dividend investors additional opportunities for income generation through premium collection from options contracts. By selling covered calls or cash-secured puts, investors can supplement dividend income and enhance overall portfolio yield.
- **Risk Management**: Options strategies provide dividend investors with tools for managing risk and protecting portfolio value. Strategies such as covered calls and dividend collar trades enable investors to hedge against downside risk while maintaining exposure to dividend-paying stocks.
- **Portfolio Diversification**: Options strategies offer dividend investors alternative approaches to portfolio management and diversification. By incorporating options strategies alongside

traditional stock holdings, investors can enhance portfolio flexibility and adapt to changing market conditions.

Considerations for Options Strategies

Risk vs. Reward: Options strategies involve inherent risks, including the potential for loss of capital and assignment of stock. Investors should carefully assess the risk-reward profile of each options strategy and consider their investment objectives, risk tolerance, and market outlook before implementing options trades.

Liquidity and Execution: Options markets may exhibit lower liquidity and wider bid-ask spreads compared to stock markets, particularly for less actively traded option contracts. Investors should consider liquidity and execution risks when entering and exiting options positions to avoid adverse price impacts.

Education and Experience: Options trading requires a solid understanding of options mechanics, pricing dynamics, and strategies. Investors should educate themselves on options trading concepts and strategies and consider gaining experience through paper trading or simulated platforms before engaging in live options trading.

By incorporating options strategies such as covered calls, cash-secured puts, and dividend collar trades into their investment arsenal, dividend investors can optimize portfolio performance and achieve their investment objectives more effectively. However, options trading involves risks and complexities that require careful consideration and ongoing education. With proper understanding, discipline, and risk management, options strategies can complement dividend investing strategies and enhance overall investment outcomes.

6.4 Real Estate Investment Trusts (REITs) and Master Limited Partnerships (MLPs)

Real Estate Investment Trusts (REITs) and Master Limited Partnerships (MLPs) are specialized investment vehicles that offer unique opportunities for income-oriented investors. In this section, we'll explore the characteristics of REITs and MLPs, their benefits for dividend investors, and considerations for incorporating them into your investment portfolio.

Real Estate Investment Trusts (REITs)

Real Estate Investment Trusts (REITs) are companies that own, operate, or finance income-producing real estate across various sectors such as residential, commercial, industrial, and healthcare. REITs are required by law to distribute a significant portion of their taxable income to shareholders in the form of dividends, making them attractive investments for income-oriented investors. Key features of REITs include:

- **High Dividend Yields**: REITs typically offer above-average dividend yields compared to other equities, thanks to their tax-advantaged status and income-generating nature.
- **Diversification**: REITs provide investors with exposure to diversified real estate assets and property types, allowing for portfolio diversification and risk mitigation.
- **Liquidity**: REITs trade on public stock exchanges like regular stocks, providing investors with liquidity and ease of access to real

estate investments without the need to directly purchase physical properties.

Master Limited Partnerships (MLPs)

Master Limited Partnerships (MLPs) are publicly traded partnerships that operate in the energy, natural resources, and infrastructure sectors. MLPs are structured as pass-through entities, meaning they distribute the majority of their income to unitholders in the form of quarterly distributions. Key features of MLPs include:

- **High Distribution Yields**: MLPs offer attractive distribution yields, often exceeding those of traditional dividend-paying stocks, due to their pass-through tax structure and cash flow generation from energy-related assets.
- **Tax Advantages**: MLPs offer tax advantages to investors, including the ability to defer taxes on distributions until units are sold and the potential for tax-deferred growth through return of capital distributions.
- **Exposure to the Energy Sector**: MLPs provide investors with exposure to the energy sector, including midstream infrastructure assets such as pipelines, storage facilities, and transportation networks, which are essential for the transportation and processing of oil, natural gas, and other energy products.

Considerations for Investing in REITs and MLPs

- **Yield vs. Risk**: While REITs and MLPs offer attractive distribution yields, investors should be mindful of associated risks, including interest rate sensitivity, regulatory risks, and sector-specific challenges such as changes in energy prices or property market conditions.
- **Tax Implications**: REITs and MLPs have unique tax implications that investors should understand before investing, including the treatment of distributions for tax purposes and the potential impact of unrelated business taxable income (UBTI) for tax-advantaged accounts.
- **Due Diligence**: Before investing in REITs and MLPs, investors should conduct thorough due diligence on individual companies, including assessing their financial health, asset quality, management team, and growth prospects. Additionally, investors should consider diversifying their exposure across multiple REITs and MLPs to mitigate company-specific risks.

In conclusion, Real Estate Investment Trusts (REITs) and Master Limited Partnerships (MLPs) offer dividend investors unique opportunities for income generation, portfolio diversification, and exposure to specialized sectors such as real estate and energy. By incorporating REITs and MLPs into their investment portfolios, dividend investors can enhance overall portfolio yield, mitigate risk, and capitalize on the income-generating potential of these specialized investment vehicles. However, investors should carefully consider the unique characteristics, risks, and tax implications of REITs and MLPs before investing and ensure proper diversification and due diligence to achieve their investment objectives.

6.5 Dividend ETFs and Mutual Funds

Dividend-focused Exchange-Traded Funds (ETFs) and Mutual Funds offer investors convenient and diversified ways to gain exposure to dividend-paying stocks. In this section, we'll explore the characteristics of Dividend ETFs and Mutual Funds, their benefits for investors, and considerations for incorporating them into your investment portfolio.

Dividend ETFs

Dividend ETFs are investment funds that hold a portfolio of dividend-paying stocks and trade on stock exchanges like individual stocks. These funds typically track an underlying index of dividend-paying companies, providing investors with diversified exposure to dividend stocks across various sectors and industries. Key features of Dividend ETFs include:

- **Diversification**: Dividend ETFs offer investors instant diversification by holding a basket of dividend-paying stocks across different sectors and geographic regions. This diversification helps reduce individual stock risk and portfolio volatility.
- **Income Generation**: Dividend ETFs focus on companies with a history of consistent dividend payments, providing investors with reliable income streams. These funds often have higher dividend yields compared to broad-market ETFs, making them attractive for income-oriented investors.
- **Low Costs**: Dividend ETFs typically have lower expense ratios compared to actively managed mutual funds, making them cost-effective investment vehicles. Additionally, ETFs offer intraday

trading liquidity and transparency of holdings, allowing investors to easily buy and sell shares throughout the trading day.

Dividend Mutual Funds

Dividend Mutual Funds are actively managed investment funds that invest in dividend-paying stocks to generate income and capital appreciation for investors. Unlike ETFs, Mutual Funds are priced once a day after the market closes and may have higher expense ratios due to active management. Key features of Dividend Mutual Funds include:

- **Active Management**: Dividend Mutual Funds are managed by professional portfolio managers who actively select and manage a portfolio of dividend-paying stocks. These managers may use fundamental analysis, quantitative models, and market research to identify attractive investment opportunities.
- **Diversification**: Similar to Dividend ETFs, Dividend Mutual Funds offer investors diversified exposure to dividend-paying stocks across various sectors and industries. The active management approach allows portfolio managers to adjust holdings based on market conditions and investment opportunities.
- **Income Focus**: Dividend Mutual Funds prioritize income generation for investors by investing in companies with a history of consistent dividend payments. These funds may also employ strategies such as dividend growth investing or sector rotation to enhance income potential and total return.

Considerations for Investing in Dividend ETFs and Mutual Funds

- **Investment Objectives**: Before investing in Dividend ETFs or Mutual Funds, investors should consider their investment objectives, risk tolerance, and time horizon. Dividend-focused funds may be suitable for income-oriented investors seeking reliable income streams and long-term capital appreciation.
- **Expense Ratios**: Compare the expense ratios of Dividend ETFs and Mutual Funds to ensure cost-effectiveness. Lower expense ratios translate to higher net returns for investors over time, especially for long-term investments.
- **Performance and Track Record**: Evaluate the historical performance and track record of Dividend ETFs and Mutual Funds, including total return, dividend yield, and volatility. Consider funds with consistent performance and experienced management teams.
- **Tax Considerations**: Understand the tax implications of investing in Dividend ETFs and Mutual Funds, including the treatment of dividends, capital gains distributions, and tax efficiency of the fund structure.

In conclusion, Dividend ETFs and Mutual Funds offer investors efficient and diversified ways to gain exposure to dividend-paying stocks. Whether you prefer the low-cost, passive approach of Dividend ETFs or the active management and potential outperformance of Dividend Mutual Funds, these investment vehicles can play a valuable role in achieving your investment objectives. By carefully evaluating the characteristics, costs, and performance of Dividend ETFs and Mutual Funds, investors can construct well-diversified portfolios and capitalize on the income-generating potential of dividend-paying stocks.

Chapter 7: Case Studies and Real-World Examples

Welcome to Chapter 7, where we dive into real-world case studies and examples to illustrate the principles and strategies discussed throughout this book. In this chapter, we'll explore actual scenarios and success stories from dividend investors, providing insights, lessons learned, and practical applications for readers.

Case Study 1: Building a Dividend Growth Portfolio

In this case study, we'll follow the journey of Sarah, a young investor with a long-term investment horizon and a goal of building a dividend growth portfolio for retirement. Sarah starts by researching Dividend Aristocrats, selecting companies with a history of consistent dividend increases. She diversifies her portfolio across sectors such as consumer staples, healthcare, and technology, focusing on companies with strong fundamentals and sustainable business models. Over time, Sarah reinvests dividends and adds new dividend-paying stocks to her portfolio, steadily increasing her dividend income and portfolio value.

Case Study 2: Generating Passive Income with REITs

In this case study, we'll examine the experience of David, a retiree seeking reliable passive income to support his living expenses. David invests in Real Estate Investment Trusts (REITs), attracted by their high dividend yields and income-generating potential. He diversifies his REIT holdings across sectors such as retail, office, and healthcare, focusing on REITs with stable cash flows and attractive valuations. By reinvesting dividends and leveraging the tax advantages of REITs, David generates a steady stream of passive income to supplement his retirement income.

Case Study 3: Hedging Risk with Options Strategies

In this case study, we'll learn from Mark, an experienced investor who uses options strategies to hedge risk and enhance income in his dividend portfolio. Mark sells covered calls against his existing stock holdings to generate additional income and protect against downside risk. He also employs cash-secured puts to enter positions in dividend-paying stocks at attractive prices, leveraging market volatility to his advantage. By implementing options strategies alongside his dividend investments, Mark effectively manages risk and enhances overall portfolio performance.

Real-World Examples: Success Stories and Lessons Learned

In addition to case studies, we'll explore real-world examples of successful dividend investors, including well-known individuals and institutional investors. We'll examine their investment philosophies, strategies, and best practices, highlighting key lessons learned and actionable insights for readers. From legendary investors like Warren Buffett to everyday investors achieving financial independence through dividend investing, these real-world examples inspire and educate readers on the potential of dividend investing to build wealth over time.

In conclusion, case studies and real-world examples offer valuable insights and practical applications for dividend investors of all levels. By studying the experiences of successful investors and learning from real-life scenarios, readers can gain confidence, knowledge, and inspiration to apply dividend investing principles and strategies to their investment journey. Whether you're building a dividend growth portfolio, generating passive income with REITs, or hedging risk with options strategies, the lessons and examples in this chapter provide a roadmap for achieving your investment goals and financial success.

7.1 Success Stories of Dividend Investors

In this section, we'll explore inspiring success stories of dividend investors who have achieved remarkable results through their dedication, discipline, and strategic approach to dividend investing. These real-life examples demonstrate the power of dividend investing to generate passive income, build wealth, and achieve financial independence.

Success Story 1: Warren Buffett

Warren Buffett, often regarded as one of the greatest investors of all time, has built his fortune through a disciplined investment approach that includes a focus on dividend-paying stocks. Buffett's conglomerate, Berkshire Hathaway, holds significant stakes in dividend-paying companies such as Coca-Cola, Apple, and Bank of America. By reinvesting dividends and holding onto high-quality dividend stocks for the long term, Buffett has generated consistent returns and built a vast fortune over several decades.

Success Story 2: John and Jane Doe

John and Jane Doe, a middle-class couple with modest savings, embarked on their journey to financial independence through dividend investing. They started by building a diversified portfolio of dividend-paying stocks across different sectors and industries, focusing on companies with strong fundamentals and sustainable dividend yields. Over time, John and Jane reinvested dividends and added new dividend stocks to their portfolio, steadily increasing their passive income stream. Through disciplined saving, prudent investing, and the power of compounding, John and Jane achieved financial independence and retired comfortably, relying on their dividend income to cover living expenses and enjoy their retirement years.

Success Story 3: The Smith Family

The Smith family, a multi-generational household, passed down the tradition of dividend investing from one generation to the next. Starting with modest investments in dividend-paying stocks, the Smith family gradually expanded their portfolio over the years, reinvesting dividends and compounding their wealth. Each generation added its own contributions to the family's investment portfolio, creating a legacy of financial security and prosperity. Today, the Smith family enjoys a substantial passive income stream from their dividend investments, providing financial stability and opportunities for future generations.

Success Story 4: Institutional Investors

Institutional investors such as pension funds, endowments, and insurance companies have long recognized the value of dividend investing for generating stable returns and meeting long-term obligations. These institutional investors allocate significant portions of their portfolios to dividend-paying stocks, leveraging the power of compounding and income generation to achieve their investment objectives. By diversifying across sectors, geographies, and asset classes, institutional investors harness the benefits of dividend investing to preserve capital, mitigate risk, and deliver consistent returns to their stakeholders.

These success stories of dividend investors illustrate the transformative impact of dividend investing on individuals, families, and institutions alike. Whether it's Warren Buffett's legendary wealth accumulation, the Doe family's journey to financial independence, the Smith family's multi-generational legacy, or the institutional investors' prudent allocation strategies, these examples underscore the timeless principles and proven benefits of dividend investing. By following in the footsteps of successful dividend investors and adopting a disciplined, long-term approach to investing, readers can unlock the full potential of dividend stocks to achieve their financial goals and secure their financial future.

7.2 Analysis of Famous Dividend Stocks

In this section, we'll conduct a comprehensive analysis of some famous dividend-paying stocks, examining their financial performance, dividend history, and investment potential. By dissecting the characteristics and prospects of these renowned companies, investors can gain valuable insights into the factors driving dividend growth and sustainability.

Company 1: Coca-Cola Company (KO)

- **Financial Performance**: Coca-Cola is a global beverage giant with a strong track record of revenue growth, profitability, and cash flow generation. The company's diversified product portfolio, brand strength, and extensive distribution network contribute to its consistent financial performance.
- **Dividend History**: Coca-Cola has a remarkable history of dividend payments, having increased its dividend for over 50 consecutive years. The company's commitment to returning capital to shareholders through dividends underscores its stability and shareholder-friendly policies.
- **Investment Potential**: Coca-Cola's strong brand, global presence, and resilient business model position it as a compelling investment for dividend investors. Despite challenges in the beverage industry, Coca-Cola's focus on innovation, diversification, and cost management bodes well for future dividend growth and capital appreciation.

Company 2: Johnson & Johnson (JNJ)

- **Financial Performance**: Johnson & Johnson is a diversified healthcare conglomerate with leading positions in pharmaceuticals, medical devices, and consumer health products. The company's robust revenue streams, R&D pipeline, and global reach contribute to its consistent financial performance and resilience.
- **Dividend History**: Johnson & Johnson is a Dividend Aristocrat with a track record of over 50 consecutive years of dividend increases. The company's commitment to innovation, operational

excellence, and prudent capital allocation supports its ability to sustain and grow dividends over time.

- **Investment Potential**: Johnson & Johnson's diversified business segments, strong brand portfolio, and focus on healthcare innovation make it an attractive investment for dividend investors. With an aging population driving demand for healthcare products and services, Johnson & Johnson is well-positioned for long-term dividend growth and shareholder value creation.

Company 3: Microsoft Corporation (MSFT)

- **Financial Performance**: Microsoft is a leading technology company with dominant positions in software, cloud computing, and productivity solutions. The company's consistent revenue growth, profitability, and cash flow generation reflect its strong competitive advantages and innovation capabilities.
- **Dividend History**: Microsoft has rapidly grown its dividend in recent years, reflecting its transition to a more mature and shareholder-friendly business model. While not a Dividend Aristocrat, Microsoft's commitment to returning capital to shareholders through dividends and share buybacks signals its confidence in future cash flow generation.
- **Investment Potential**: Microsoft's leadership in cloud computing, artificial intelligence, and digital transformation positions it as a compelling investment for dividend investors seeking exposure to the technology sector. With a diverse revenue base, recurring subscription model, and strong balance sheet, Microsoft has ample room for future dividend growth and capital appreciation.

These analyses of famous dividend-paying stocks highlight the diverse opportunities available to dividend investors across different sectors and industries. Companies like Coca-Cola, Johnson & Johnson, and Microsoft exemplify the qualities of stable, shareholder-friendly businesses with a commitment to dividend growth and sustainability. By conducting thorough analyses of these companies' financial performance, dividend histories, and investment potential, investors can make informed decisions and construct well-diversified dividend portfolios aligned with their investment objectives and risk tolerance.

7.3 Lessons from Dividend Investing Mistakes

In this section, we'll explore valuable lessons learned from common dividend investing mistakes, highlighting pitfalls to avoid and strategies to mitigate risk. By examining the experiences of investors who have encountered challenges in dividend investing, readers can gain insights into best practices and principles for building successful dividend portfolios.

Mistake 1: Chasing High Yields without Due Diligence

Lesson Learned: One common mistake in dividend investing is chasing high yields without conducting thorough due diligence on the underlying companies. While high dividend yields may appear attractive on the surface, they could signal underlying risks such as unsustainable payout ratios, deteriorating fundamentals, or impending dividend cuts. Investors should prioritize quality over yield, focusing on companies with strong financials, sustainable business models, and a history of consistent dividend growth.

Mistake 2: Neglecting Dividend Sustainability and Growth

Lesson Learned: Another mistake is neglecting to assess the sustainability and growth potential of dividends. Some investors focus solely on current dividend yield without considering factors such as earnings growth, cash flow stability, and dividend payout ratios. It's essential to evaluate a company's ability to maintain and grow dividends over time, taking into account industry dynamics, competitive positioning, and management quality. By prioritizing dividends with a track record of growth and a clear path to sustainability, investors can build resilient portfolios capable of weathering market volatility and economic cycles.

Mistake 3: Overlooking Diversification and Risk Management

Lesson Learned: Diversification and risk management are critical aspects of successful dividend investing that investors should not overlook. Concentrating investments in a few high-yield stocks or sectors exposes investors to elevated risks, including company-specific and sector-specific factors. By diversifying across different sectors, industries, and asset classes, investors can spread risk and mitigate the impact of adverse events on their portfolios. Additionally, employing risk management techniques such as stop-loss orders, position sizing, and portfolio rebalancing can help investors protect capital and preserve wealth over the long term.

Mistake 4: Ignoring Tax Implications and Portfolio Allocation

Lesson Learned: Ignoring tax implications and portfolio allocation can be detrimental to dividend investors' long-term success. Different types of dividends (qualified vs. non-qualified) are subject to varying tax rates, which can significantly impact after-tax returns. Investors should consider tax-efficient investment vehicles such as qualified dividend stocks, tax-advantaged accounts (e.g., IRAs, 401(k)s), and tax-loss harvesting strategies to minimize tax liabilities and maximize after-tax income. Additionally, maintaining a well-balanced portfolio allocation that aligns with investment objectives, risk tolerance, and time horizon is crucial for achieving diversification and long-term financial goals.

Mistake 5: Emotional Investing and Short-Term Thinking

Lesson Learned: Emotional investing and short-term thinking can lead to impulsive decisions and suboptimal outcomes in dividend investing. Investors may panic-sell during market downturns, chase hot trends, or succumb to fear and greed, resulting in missed opportunities and underperformance. It's essential to maintain discipline, patience, and a long-term perspective when investing in dividend stocks, focusing on fundamentals, quality, and intrinsic value rather than short-term price movements. By adhering to a well-defined investment strategy, remaining resilient in the face of market volatility, and staying committed to long-term goals, investors can navigate the ups and downs of dividend investing with confidence and conviction.

In conclusion, dividend investing mistakes provide valuable learning opportunities for investors to refine their strategies, enhance their decision-making process, and achieve better outcomes over time. By avoiding common pitfalls such as chasing high yields, neglecting dividend sustainability, overlooking diversification, ignoring tax implications, and succumbing to emotional biases, investors can build resilient dividend portfolios capable of generating sustainable income and long-term wealth. By embracing lessons from past mistakes and applying sound principles of dividend investing, investors can navigate the complexities of the market with confidence and achieve their financial goals with greater success.

7.4 Building a Sample Dividend Portfolio

In this section, we'll construct a sample dividend portfolio comprising a diversified selection of dividend-paying stocks across different sectors and industries. The goal of this sample portfolio is to demonstrate a balanced approach to dividend investing, focusing on quality, sustainability, and long-term growth potential.

Portfolio Allocation:

- Consumer Staples: 25%
- Healthcare: 20%
- Technology: 20%
- Utilities: 15%
- Financials: 10%
- Industrials: 10%

Sample Dividend Stocks:

1. Consumer Staples (25%):

The Procter & Gamble Company (PG): A leading consumer goods company with a diversified portfolio of household and personal care products. PG has a long history of consistent dividend increases and strong brand recognition.

2. Healthcare (20%):

Johnson & Johnson (JNJ): A diversified healthcare company engaged in pharmaceuticals, medical devices, and consumer health products. JNJ is a Dividend Aristocrat with a track record of over 50 consecutive years of dividend increases.

3. Technology (20%):

Microsoft Corporation (MSFT): A global technology leader providing software, cloud computing, and productivity solutions. MSFT has rapidly grown its dividend in recent years and offers exposure to the fast-growing tech sector.

4. Utilities (15%):

NextEra Energy, Inc. (NEE): A leading clean energy utility company with a focus on renewable energy generation and transmission. NEE offers stable dividends supported by regulated operations and long-term growth prospects in the renewable energy sector.

5. Financials (10%):

JPMorgan Chase & Co. (JPM): A leading financial services firm offering a wide range of banking, investment, and wealth management services. JPM has a solid dividend history and benefits from its diversified business model and strong market position.

6. Industrials (10%):

3M Company (MMM): A diversified industrial conglomerate with operations in healthcare, consumer, and industrial markets. MMM has a track record of dividend growth and innovation, supported by its global presence and diversified revenue streams.

Portfolio Management:

- **Dividend Reinvestment**: Reinvest dividends from each stock back into the respective companies to compound returns over time and accelerate wealth accumulation.
- **Regular Monitoring**: Continuously monitor the financial performance and dividend sustainability of each stock in the portfolio, adjusting holdings as needed based on changing market conditions and investment objectives.

- **Diversification**: Maintain a well-diversified portfolio across sectors and industries to spread risk and mitigate exposure to company-specific or sector-specific factors.
- **Long-Term Perspective**: Adopt a long-term investment horizon and resist the urge to make impulsive decisions based on short-term market fluctuations. Focus on the fundamentals of each company and the overall portfolio strategy.

By following this sample dividend portfolio construction, investors can build a well-diversified portfolio of quality dividend-paying stocks aligned with their investment objectives and risk tolerance. By selecting companies with strong financials, sustainable dividends, and long-term growth potential across different sectors and industries, investors can generate reliable income, preserve capital, and achieve long-term wealth accumulation through dividend investing. Remember to conduct thorough due diligence, stay disciplined in portfolio management, and maintain a long-term perspective to maximize the benefits of dividend investing over time.

7.5 Future Trends in Dividend Investing

In this section, we'll explore emerging trends and developments shaping the future of dividend investing. From technological advancements to demographic shifts, these trends offer insights into the evolving landscape of dividend investing and the opportunities and challenges that lie ahead.

Trend 1: Growth of ESG Investing

Environmental, Social, and Governance (ESG) investing has gained traction in recent years, driven by increasing awareness of sustainability issues and the integration of ESG factors into investment decisions. Dividend investors are placing greater emphasis on companies with strong ESG practices, viewing them as indicators of long-term sustainability and responsible corporate stewardship. As ESG considerations become mainstream in investment analysis, dividend investors may prioritize companies with favorable ESG profiles, contributing to a shift towards more sustainable dividend investing strategies.

Trend 2: Rise of Technology and Digital Transformation

The rapid pace of technological innovation and digital transformation is reshaping industries and business models, presenting both opportunities and challenges for dividend investors. Companies leveraging technology to drive growth, enhance efficiency, and adapt to changing consumer preferences may offer attractive investment opportunities for dividend investors. Additionally, dividend-paying technology companies, once perceived as growth-oriented and non-dividend payers, are increasingly returning capital to shareholders through dividends and share buybacks, reflecting their maturation and cash-generating capabilities.

Trend 3: Demographic Shifts and Aging Population

Demographic shifts, including an aging population and changing consumer preferences, are influencing dividend investing trends. As the baby boomer generation enters retirement, there is a growing demand for income-generating investments to fund living expenses and retirement savings. Dividend-paying stocks, particularly those with reliable income streams and sustainable dividends, are appealing to retirees and income-oriented investors seeking reliable income in a low-interest-rate environment. Additionally, companies catering to the needs of aging populations, such as healthcare and consumer staples, may benefit from demographic tailwinds and offer attractive investment opportunities for dividend investors.

Trend 4: Focus on Dividend Growth and Quality

Amid economic uncertainty and market volatility, dividend investors are placing greater emphasis on dividend growth and quality. Companies with a history of consistent dividend increases, strong financials, and resilient business models are favored by dividend investors seeking stability and income growth. Dividend Aristocrats, companies with a track record of 25 or more consecutive years of dividend increases, are particularly sought after for their proven ability to navigate economic downturns and deliver reliable income and capital appreciation over the long term.

Trend 5: Evolution of Dividend ETFs and Funds

Dividend-focused Exchange-Traded Funds (ETFs) and mutual funds are evolving to meet the changing needs of dividend investors. With the rise of passive investing and factor-based strategies, dividend ETFs and funds are offering innovative approaches to dividend investing, including smart beta strategies, thematic investing, and factor tilts. Additionally, the proliferation of dividend ETFs and funds focused on specific themes such as sustainable dividends, high yield, or dividend growth provides investors with a range of options to tailor their dividend portfolios to their investment objectives and risk preferences.

The future of dividend investing is shaped by a convergence of trends and developments, including the growth of ESG investing, technological innovation, demographic shifts, and evolving investor preferences. By staying attuned to these trends and incorporating them into their investment strategies, dividend investors can adapt to changing market conditions, capitalize on emerging opportunities, and achieve long-term success in generating reliable income and building wealth through dividend investing. With a focus on dividend growth, quality, and sustainability, investors can navigate the evolving landscape of dividend investing with confidence and conviction.

Conclusion:

Congratulations on concluding "Dividend Stocks: A Complete Guide to Investing in High-Yield Stocks for Long-Term Financial Success and Growing Your Portfolio to Generate Passive Income." Throughout this comprehensive guide, we've explored the timeless principles, strategies, and techniques for harnessing the power of dividend investing to achieve your financial goals and build wealth over the long term.

In this journey, we've delved into the fundamentals of dividend investing, understanding the importance of dividends as a source of passive income and the role they play in driving long-term total returns. We've learned how to identify high-quality dividend-paying stocks, conduct thorough research and analysis, and construct well-diversified portfolios aligned with our investment objectives and risk tolerance.

We've examined the various types of dividend stocks, from Dividend Aristocrats with a proven track record of dividend increases to high-yield dividend stocks offering attractive income opportunities. We've explored the benefits of dividend reinvestment, compounding returns, and the power of patience and discipline in achieving financial success through dividend investing.

We've discussed the importance of risk management, portfolio diversification, and maintaining a long-term perspective amidst market volatility and economic uncertainty. We've recognized the evolving trends and developments shaping the future of dividend investing, from the rise of ESG investing to the impact of technological innovation and demographic shifts on investment strategies.

As you embark on your dividend investing journey, remember the key principles and lessons shared in this guide:

- Prioritize quality over yield, focusing on companies with strong fundamentals, sustainable dividends, and a history of consistent dividend growth.
- Conduct thorough due diligence and research before investing, understanding the financial health, business model, and growth prospects of each company in your portfolio.
- Diversify your portfolio across sectors, industries, and asset classes to spread risk and mitigate exposure to market fluctuations.
- Embrace a long-term perspective, resisting the temptation to make impulsive decisions based on short-term market movements, and focusing on the fundamentals of each company and the overall portfolio strategy.

By applying these principles and techniques, you can navigate the complexities of the market with confidence and achieve your financial goals through dividend investing. Whether you're seeking to supplement your income, build wealth for retirement, or achieve financial independence, dividend stocks offer a proven path to long-term financial success and passive income generation.

Thank you for embarking on this journey with us. May your dividend investing endeavors be fruitful, rewarding, and filled with long-term prosperity and financial well-being.

Happy investing!